GET OFF THE CURB

A Healthy Rebellion from Fight or Flight
to Activated Achiever

LAUREN DANIELLE

Positively Powered Publications
PO Box 270098
Louisville, CO 80027
positivelypoweredpublications.com

Editor: Amy Collette
Cover Design: Melody Christian

Get Off The Curb/Lauren Danielle. 1st ed.
ISBN 978-1-7329022-8-2

*To those who inspired this book
and those who will be inspired by it.*

~ LAUREN DANIELLE

CONTENTS

INTRODUCTION: To You, From Me. With Love

Hey there. It's Lauren. Kicked to the curb, bullied to bully, drugs and alcohol, food addiction, poor relationships, lies, betrayal, loss, and grief. All of this led to a massive lack of trust, constantly feeling misunderstood, anxious, temperamental, and defensive. Simply put, I was always ready to fight, and if I couldn't fight, I was ready to run. When I look back, it's easy to see how life could have taken me down a completely different path; however, with hard work, relentless focus, self-love, and grit, I became the person I was meant to be, not the person my excuses could have allowed me to be.

The people in my story are not ordinary. They all have an impact on me. Through the good and bad experiences, they taught me valuable lessons. These individuals are my parents, siblings, teachers, extended family members, coaches, mentors, therapists, friends, and my exes. So many people have left an impression on my heart and played a role in who I am today.

I'll give you a heads-up: this isn't a pretty story to tell. In fact, it's messy, super messy in some parts, but it's my story and in some ways, there's a good chance it is your story too. We often see someone's glory, but we don't always know the story behind it.

My message to you is that no life event is worth delaying living your purpose, and there's not one person who should dull your sparkle! Remember, the sun always shines after it rains. Even when we can't see through the fog, I believe we need to know that everything happens for a reason, and with a positive mindset and resilient heart, everything will always be just fine.

There's a chance you're hearing a number of stories in your head...

"You'll never be good enough."

"You'll always be a screw-up!"

"Who would ever want you?"

"Why are you the way you are?"

That last question? Yep, that's the one I want you to hold on to because it's the thread of love I want you to follow with me through this book.

For years, I was misunderstood. I was a rebel, an outsider, part of the "I just don't care" crowd. It sabotaged so many of my relationships, family life, friendships, and even what I was looking for in love.

Chances are you already see yourself in this story. As you read my story, it may bring up Christmas memories you don't want to talk about. It may trigger feelings of how someone made you feel. You may experience emotions you didn't know were still residing inside of you.

Maybe it's that one conversation still ringing in your ears that you can't let go of. I'm writing this to give you hope, to show you possibilities, and to remind you that you were created on purpose... with purpose... and to never let anyone dull your sparkle! I am going to show you what wasn't always easy, but looking back, was all worth it.

You are enough.

That phrase may be hard to read right now, and be honest, it's OK if you even smirked while reading that line. I've been there. Whether your heart jumped or your face scowled, I want that truth to stick: you are enough.

You are lovable. You are worthy. You are enough. The fact that you're still reading this gives me hope that you're holding onto who you really want to be. I'm here to share my story about how I "got off the curb," and how you can too.

From Fight or Flight to Activated Achiever ... let's go!

XOXO
~Lauren

"YOU'RE GOING TO END UP ALONE..."

"I am sorry if I hurt you, but I want you to know that I love you. I really, really do."

March 2017. That's when life changed forever, in the best way possible. One of life's biggest wake-up calls happened, but it began with immense heartache. My older sister Rachael, who is also my best friend, was in town visiting for a weekend and our Sunday funday turned into one of the worst arguments we've ever had. While we ultimately realized it was a massive misunderstanding and even bigger miscommunication, the underlying issue was the trigger I felt that day.

I felt inferior to my sister, even unheard by her, which led to my lashing out at her. For the majority of my life, I struggled to communicate my feelings, possibly because I didn't even always understand them myself. Often, the result was a reaction, a defensiveness that not only hurt people but also pushed them away.

I'm sure you have heard the phrase that sometimes life is about breaking down before breaking through, and this conversation led me to one of the biggest turning points in my life. On Monday morning, we were sitting at my kitchen table. The energy was so tense and the level of discomfort was so high.

Rachael started sharing her thoughts and some tough-to-hear truths, such as "You can't hurt the people you love, Lauren. The things you're saying are cruel and ruthless."

Even though I was feeling apologetic and empathetic, and I knew I would never deliberately hurt her. I couldn't hide from the fact that I had deeply hurt her. I also knew there was a much bigger reason that caused my rebellious and extreme temper outburst.

We continued the conversation, trying to see each other's point of view and make amends, but ultimately, we were going in circles of minuscule details. What she said next stopped me dead in my tracks and shook me to my core—a feeling I had never experienced and can vividly recall today.

"I think you're incapable of a healthy relationship, and my fear is that you're going to end up alone because of how you treat people."

****

When I was much younger, I often found myself alone sitting on the curb outside my house or other places away from my family. That was my safe place, my spot where I could be far enough away. As an adult, I found myself in the same type of emotional territory, even if the location and circumstances were different.

I became accustomed to that cold feeling of isolation, not feeling understood, the urge to self-protect, and a loneliness that couldn't be described because no one knew how sensitive I really was on the inside. Not only was my emotional isolation hurting *me*, but it was hurting others.

I didn't realize how much I was pushing others away, or how little I let them in, and I knew that if something was going to change, I needed to change. I have always been one to look at myself in the mirror before I start pointing fingers, and I knew I needed to get up and get off the curb, once and for all. Otherwise, I dreaded a lonely, frustrating future.

My sister is a health psychologist, and I usually was not a fan when I felt she was analyzing me or going through the role of conflict resolution, but sometimes she was so spot on, and so accurate, it was hard to not hear what she had to say

It was difficult at times not to receive her advice, even when I felt it was unwarranted. For most of my life, at the drop of a hat, I had a hair-trigger internal switch where I got defensive, and in seconds was literally like an animal that could attack or I wanted to run and hide to get as far away as possible. From the outside, people saw my emotions as irrational or unjustified, and, while I couldn't always explain why I reacted the way I did, I knew that I wasn't upset without reason.

It took me years before I learned it was because I did not innately trust people, and therefore, was constantly self-protecting. This conversation with Rachael was not very long because it only took one sentence to really shake me. More than that though, for the first time ever, as much as what she said hurt, it was a scary thought to think I would never fall in love.

I knew she was not trying to hurt me. The puppy dog tears in my sister's eyes and her quivering lip were more than enough to remind me she wasn't trying to hurt me at all. She was giving me the gift of truth, and tough love, because of how much she really cares.

I knew in my heart how loving I really was and that my intentions would never be to hurt someone, but I also knew that no one understood why I got defensive, why I instinctively self-protected. I'm not even sure I knew why then, but I was committed to figuring it out.

A popular adage that's led me time and time again is, "If something is going to change, then something has to change." I decided right then I would do *whatever* it took to get to the root cause of my triggers. I determined to change the narrative and my reactions to those I love, to find my worth and attract the man of my dreams, and ultimately, become the best version of me.

That was when I decided to *get off the curb!*

Catalyst for Change

I was a reluctant leader. It took me *years* before I stepped into a leadership role, and even more years before I put all the puzzle pieces of my leadership potential together. Now, I see I was *born* to be a leader! This is my purpose, passion, and calling for life.

I've always believed in the adages "everything happens for a reason" and "everything has led to where you are supposed to be right now," but I didn't necessarily believe they applied to my potential. I went through several experiences of trying to learn how to relate to others, empathize better, and more importantly, help others make a shift. I remember finding my drive in college. It was probably when my activator or achiever *strengths* kicked on, and, I can recall wanting to always improve, and having this innate sense of wanting to grow and strive for more; however, I didn't realize my experiences could also relate to others, or better yet, motivate them. At the time, I was in this space of proving something to someone, maybe myself, maybe others who doubted me and wasn't aware that my own pursuit could also impact others.

So many inspirational leaders have shaped my life and continue to shape my future. Tony Robbins, Les Brown, Lisa Nichols, and Jay Shetty are just a few, but I can remember thinking, *They all started from somewhere, they all have their own individual story and life-shaping events. Each of these individuals has a unique past and they did not experience overnight success.*

There was a time when people kept saying, "Lauren, you need to share your story, people have no idea what you have experienced," or "Lauren, you provide belief of what is possible for others and you get people into action in a way I've never seen," but instead of focusing on what I was doing for someone else, I was too afraid of what people would think of me. When I wanted to offer coaching advice, I kept quiet.

When I wanted to empower others, I feared judgment. When I wanted to help others, I worried people would think I was doing it for my benefit, and not for theirs and, in turn, I shied away from sharing my story for a long time.

As I started to have gratitude for the motivational leaders I follow, and an understanding that their vulnerability was so much of who I was becoming, I truly felt a connection because of similar feelings or experiences. I knew I was doing others a disservice by not sharing, not having a voice, and not taking a stance.

Now, I am certain my life experiences and *strengths* allow me to step up to the moment of impact. It is the *Challenger* in me who demands the truth, refuses manipulation, addresses conflict, or confronts what is off so we can make it right. When you combine a strong personality with incredibly challenging life experiences and a vision of what is possible, that's the recipe for rising up to greatness. I know what's igniting me to rise up, to want to help others, and to find a way for others to live in freedom and break free of the stories, pain, and patterns holding them back.

Personal Growth Journey

I have been a self-help junkie for over two decades now. It's been a burning desire to surround myself with successful and driven individuals, but I also committed to take action, implement what I learn, get better, and grow, not simply be inspired. It's one thing to listen to a podcast or attend a conference, and it is another to begin to apply it. Put another way, looking at *Muscle & Fitness* magazines is not going to get the same results as putting yourself through those grueling workouts.

We tend to idealize certain people, celebrities in the eyes of some, without acknowledging or seeing all the work they did to reach that status (the story behind the glory). When I think about some of the most influential voices in the world, I can also recall their hardships, those experiences that shaped so much of their trajectory. Many of us would look at them and be inspired or even think they just got lucky, when in actuality, they mastered their mindsets, overcame incredible challenges and hardships, and decided to revolutionize their lives instead of settling for the cards they were originally dealt.

Part of this book, what's catching your eyes right now, is where I want to share some of the takeaways learned from podcasts, books, or seminars and how they truly impacted me. I want you to consider how these messages can also impact you.

One major common denominator is that we *all* have a story. When we slow down, listen, and ask questions, it's fascinating to see how each of us overcame obstacles, faced difficulties, and found someone who believes in us.

While our stories are unique and do not *define* us, they surely do shape us. I remember when I first starting sharing my story, and I would tell myself, *Who cares, Lauren? No one is going to want to hear this!*

To my surprise, the opposite started to happen. I was so humbled and gratefully shocked that people were not only interested but also inspired. That was when I committed to sharing my story to connect with others, to help people. I started on my mission: encouraging others to speak up and share their stories as well. Our experiences and vulnerability are often the foundation of human connection and relationships. That commonality is where my personal growth journey led me to be a catalyst for change.

Cracking the Code with Lisa

Everything happens for a reason, and the timing of what happens is as important as what happens. Just a few weeks prior to the incident with Rachael, a good friend suggested I connect with Lisa Foster, a life coach. My friend assured me that Lisa's *Free to Shine* program was exactly what I needed.

At the time, I was resistant, incredibly resistant actually. My friend saw where I was struggling with self-worth, and even more so, she noticed where I was struggling to find the man of my dreams. My issue was more than just attracting a decent man because I was becoming accustomed to cheaters and liars; it was also about maintaining a healthy relationship once I met someone wonderful.

She was confident Lisa could assist me. No surprise, I had my guard up and thought I had already done plenty of work on myself. I had hired many coaches and therapists in the past, and I didn't have the desire to go down that path again. I always seemed to end up at the same place: completely misunderstood with no real change in behavior or outcome.

After the incredibly upsetting conversation with my sister, I started wondering, *What if Lisa could be someone who could 'crack the code' with me? What if Lisa is the ticket to me escaping my fight or flight response behavior?*

What if Lisa could actually help me transform into the person I am on the inside that I was never capable of correctly expressing on the outside? What if she is the one coach I hadn't met yet that who could 'get' me, and therefore allow me to be the person I've always wanted to be? The person buried deep inside of fear, pain, sadness, and doubt.

I have a huge heart. While others perceive me as tough or strong, deep inside I am quite sensitive, not as resilient as I may appear, and was carrying a lot of pain that I was projecting in toxic ways.

I didn't understand why I couldn't explain how I was feeling, why I was always felt misunderstood by others, or how much I was actually self-protecting, but I was committed to figuring it out. I knew I spent too much time being so concerned with what others thought of me or putting up barriers.

I was too afraid of getting hurt, which was preventing me from showing up as the girl full of love, with a free-spirited inner child. Instead, I was showing up jaded, defensive, and ready to aggressively stand up for myself or run away at any moment.

Regardless of how small or large of an event, I lived in a place where I felt high strung, was always ready to fight, and never fully let people in. In short, I never really trusted. At the end of the day, it was hurting me more than anyone else, and good people were paying the price for what others had done, when in actuality they were not deserving of my ruthless and distant heart.

I made the decision to call Lisa, and I can recall nearly interrogating her about what she does, how she could help me, and what made her *different* from everyone else out there. I wish I could recollect her exact comments to me, but even though I can't recall her precise words, the way Lisa made me feel was something I had never experienced before and will never forget.

For probably the first time ever, I felt completely heard, completely unjudged, and completely understood. Almost instantaneously, I was calm, trusting, and confident this woman was going to be my healing key. Before even meeting Lisa, I was confident she was a mentor who would give me permission to be vulnerable.

I knew that if I got real and raw and didn't just shuffle through the motions. I could actually let go of the past and step into the leader, daughter, sister, friend, and hopefully, spouse I've always wanted to be. For the first time ever, I wasn't focused on what someone was going to think of me. I focused on how to become the best version of myself.

My journey with Lisa was unlike any other health coaching, personal growth, or therapy I've ever experienced. For starters, I made a decision before I began that if I was going to hire her, I was committing to being vulnerable, truthful, defenseless, and not holding back at all. In the past, I found ways to tell my mentors or coaches what I wanted them to hear, or what I thought they wanted to hear, and not always what was actually going on. I was too afraid of what they might think of me, and I was the only one who paid the price. I stayed in a familiar cycle that wasn't serving me, but this time, I was willing to get uncomfortable as long as it yielded a different outcome.

Personal growth is not easy. Doing the work, truly facing your demons, and recognizing your patterns is incredibly challenging; however, if you don't sweep your "stuff" under the rug and you do face your reflection in the mirror, the payoff is remarkable.

I trusted Lisa. I knew she didn't come from a place of judgment, and if it was going to be, it was going to be up to me to show up differently. One aspect of her program that was different was Lisa didn't spend countless hours going down memory lane from birth to adulthood, digging up decades of details. Instead, she took the lessons, experiences, and shame from the past, to teach me how to shine, break free, forgive, and understand how and why I did what I did, and how to live differently.

The 12 intense weeks I spent coaching with Lisa unraveled so many ah-ha moments of my past. It turned on a light to illuminate my identity. I started understanding how and why I behaved a particular way or made certain decisions in my past. I also had so many ah-ha moments about what I was capable of.

I saw what the best version of me looked like when I was in a healthy state, and for the first time I also understood why I was behaving how I was. Lisa taught me about my strengths and how they not only distinguished me but also how they could hurt and hinder my life. For the first time in my 35 years, I had permission to *be*. I unapologetically found self-love for my perfectly imperfect self.

Lisa enlightened me about why control was a domineering part of my personality, but also how vulnerability and the ability to let go was going to be the gateway for me to continue to open up greatness in my life—with my business, with self-love, and most importantly, for the number one reason I hired her, my personal relationships. Looking back, I finally had clarity about who I was as a child, who I was as a teen, how I redirected my life into becoming the leader I am today, and how I could pay this forward.

You know I believe that everything happens for a reason, and every incident is setting us up for the next moment of impact. I also believe life is constantly giving us lessons and opportunities, but it is up to us to reflect, learn, and ultimately grow and evolve into the people we truly want to be—the best versions of ourselves.

Another theme I dug up was this ongoing story playing in my head of not being good enough. As a child, I rebelled because if I couldn't meet the standard or expectation, I figured I might as well not even try and took on an "I don't care" attitude. Instead of trying or giving it my all, I feared my best might still not be enough, so I chose a route where I couldn't be judged.

I was deciding not to behave instead of someone else assessing if I met a certain standard. Instead of worrying about succeeding, I just gave up and didn't have to worry about being good enough since I never even tried. Can you relate?

As an adult, I am the epitome of an overachiever. The story in my head was the same, however, the outward expression had changed. Instead of not doing anything, I was constantly going above and beyond, and even when I should be celebrating an accomplishment, I was beating myself up with a repeat record in my head of what I could've done better.

I didn't get to the root issue. I needed to recognize the core shame message that was stuck on repeat in my subconscious brain for many, many years. During that journey, I gathered numerous college degrees, including two bachelor's and two master's degrees, multitudinous fitness and continuing education certificates, and competed in many races, fitness competitions, and triathlons.

Yes, I have a competitive nature, but I achieved and competed because I felt like I had something to *prove*. No matter what I did, I always had an uneasy feeling that it wasn't enough or I could've done better. So often I wasn't enjoying what I was doing, as much as I was compensating for the void residing deep inside of me.

Now don't get me wrong. I am not one to settle for average or mediocrity, and I do believe in striving for more. On the other hand, it is also amazing when you can find gratitude in what you have and who you already are, and then, you can celebrate each successful point, progress, and personal progress breakthroughs along your journey.

Have you ever struggled with feeling good enough? Many of us struggle with core shame messages, either not feeling worthy, lovable or good enough, and often it is *learned* early in life. One of the values I am so passionate about today is busting through those limiting beliefs and self-limiting thoughts.

You are lovable. You are worthy. You are good enough!

It took me a long time and a lot of help to get to where I am today. Now, my mission and vision are paying this forward and lifting up as many others as possible along the way!

CHRISTMAS ON THE CURB: Party of One

It's Christmas Eve. The carols are playing, lights are twinkling, the tree is dressed with glittery presents, and snow is falling outside. I can imagine the smell of Mama's homemade lasagna and breaded chicken in the oven and her homemade spaghetti and meat sauce simmering in the kitchen. I can picture my little brother in his high chair at the end of the dining room table, sitting and playing as any innocent toddler would. I remember watching my sister play the piano, and I could hear the songs in my head as she tuned out most of what was going on around her. She lost herself in the rhythm of the music.

What I most remember is looking back through the living room window, watching everyone continue to go through the motions as if nothing was wrong or out of place.

Where was I? Sitting outside, alone on the curb. I will never forget the sadness, loneliness, anger, frustration, and isolation I felt as an 11-year-old girl. How in the world could my entire family just carry on with the festivities when there was a young girl, scared, sad, frustrated, and cold, sitting outside on the curb all by herself—on Christmas Eve! I remember tucking my knees into my chest and wrapping my arms around my legs to stop my stomach from shaking.

I balled my fists so tightly that it pressed my nails into my palms in pain. I so badly wanted to release the tension raging in my body and think of the most awful and angry thoughts so I would stay mad, and not feel sad. The last thing I wanted anyone to see me do was cry, which felt debilitating to me. If I was tough and angry, I felt I was in control, as if I had opted for it.

No way was I going to appear weak or allow anyone to see my hurt, so I bottled up every ounce of sadness and converted it to anger. I tried convincing myself I made this choice, as opposed to feeling like the victim of someone else's choice. Although I may have seemed or felt invisible to everyone inside the house, my lasting impression was exile, shame, and abandonment. Why didn't anyone come out to check on me or invite me back inside? I *was 11 years old!*

My parents were divorced and remarried to new spouses by that time. Mom lived in Aurora with her husband while Dad and my stepmom lived in Boulder, 45 minutes away from each other. I knew Dad was on his way, making the 45-minute drive through holiday traffic to rescue his little girl. So, I waited on the curb of the cul-de-sac, freezing and wondering, *What's wrong with me? Why do they hate me? How come no one has come to see if you are OK?* And, *does anyone even care about me?*

Christmas is supposed to be a joyful time of year, but for me, it was often the worst time. Each year from pre-teen to college I wanted to feel so happy and excited, but I walked on eggshells, never knowing when the eruption would happen. Christmas was not a time I could relax or be in the moment of the holiday spirit. At my mom's house I often experienced a room so full of tension it could shatter glass.

I lived in fear wondering when the explosion would occur, wondering how such a special and monumental holiday could erupt into such family turmoil, again and again, year after year. In seconds we could go from singing, dancing, and cooking to name-calling, taunting, button-pushing, and ultimately, the separation between my family and me.

For many people, Christmas is exciting, with family coming into town and Santa sliding down the chimney. As a very young child, that is exactly how I remember it too. We set out milk and cookies after we tracked Santa on the news. I remember Christmas movies, festive pajamas, and all the feel-good emotions.

Unfortunately, for most of my adolescent and teenage years, it was the complete opposite. From middle school on, Christmas Eve was infected with anxiety, fear, and sadness with a ticking time bomb, just waiting for those words to appear from my stepfather. "Get the f**k out of my house, Lauren!"

At moments I truly was trying to mind my own business. It was almost as if he was looking for ways to set me off; to antagonize me. No matter if I was well-behaved or not, it was only a matter of time before I ended up on the curb, divided, detached, and disconnected from the rest of the family.

What did I do to not only get kicked out year after year, but that my mom and sister didn't rescue me, let alone check on me? I used to wonder if they didn't love me enough. I used to wonder if they were afraid the outlash would get turned on them? Over time, I learned that both my mom and my sister avoid conflict so much, are the epitome of *peacemakers*, that it was easier for them to look the other way, and stay clear of the confrontation than it was to take a stance for me, to intervene in any way.

I'll be the first to admit: I had a chip on my shoulder and was the sassiest of all sassy teenagers, but even when I was minding my own business, I was a target. I was on edge and it took very little for me to snap or be combative, and yet, *no one* deserves that treatment, especially by your family, especially as a child, and *especially* on a holiday.

This was the beginning of me fighting back. This was the early stages of me never trusting with my whole heart. This was where my skepticism of people began. Most importantly, it was when my unhealthy expression of being ruthless, heartless, and defensive first showed up. I learned very early on very few were in my corner, if any at all at times. It wasn't until I found my life coach at 33 that I started to understand this change, but it's important for you to first see how unpleasant and angry a teenager I was and what *caused* that behavior.

Two Households

I grew up in a divorced family with parents who were the opposite of each other in every single way—their faiths, communication styles, parenting styles, political views; the list goes on. As kids, we had the opportunity to celebrate many different holidays, the experience of 'step' relationships and extended step-family members, commuted back and forth between homes, and juggled our time between parents.

While this may be unique or different for some, for me, this lifestyle was the only thing I knew and the only way I remember things. I don't remember the original four: my mom, my dad, my older sister Rachael, and me. I only know my parents' second relationships as well as my step and half-siblings. My parents separated before I was 2, and they both had their new life partners by the time I was 3. Their divorce finalized when I was 5 and both of my biological parents remarried. This was the only way of life I knew: mixed values, mixed parents, mixed religions, and mixed personalities. It was my real-life Brady Bunch living, except each household had a completely different vibe.

When I was a little kid, I only remember delightful and joyous times at both houses. Regardless, if we were with Dad doing Passover or Mom doing Easter, the homes were always full of tasty food, great music, and good people. On the other hand, my parents' divorce was not exactly easy, which to be completely transparent and honest, is an absolute understatement—it was a big stinking mess!

My mom was raised in a strong Catholic household in Ashland, Wisconsin. Dad grew up in a traditional Jewish neighborhood in Cleveland, Ohio. Before my parents married, and surely before my sister and I were born, my mom actually converted to Judaism; however, after the separation, she quickly reverted to Catholicism. When they divorced, the judge ruled joint custody, but my dad felt strongly that my sister Rachael and I should be raised Jewish, especially since my mom was technically Jewish when we were born. Raising us Jewish was a vision they shared before they were married.

Dad was one of the first people in the United States to ever *fight* for religious custody, and he won! The problems began when my mom was not compliant with court orders. Rachael and I were allowed by court order to go to church only on Easter and Christmas - and that's all! My mom and stepdad were taking us to Mass regularly, almost daily, including before we went to school. We went to church on Sundays, said grace every night at the table, and had crucifixes in our rooms.

I don't recall that we ever tattled, but kids are so truthful and honest, that I can imagine that's how the secret leaked, simply being asked questions about our day or week when we were with Dad. My parents' civil battle reached national news, many mainstream talk shows, including Larry King and Phil Donahue, and major newspapers, even the front page of *The New York Times* because my mom was not compliant with the courts. This, of course, led to a very catchy headline: "Mom Goes To Jail For Taking Kids To Church." She didn't actually do any jail time, but she knew she was in contempt with the court's orders. At that point, she did actually stop taking us to church, but the drama did not stop.

I remember from an early age my parents bickering over various issues, specifically my stepdad being catty and mimicking of my dad and stepmom. He mocked how "crunchy" or organic they were or found ways to try to elevate himself. He talked about the way he did things at *his* house, as if it was so much better, or made fun of or put down the way they did things at *their* house, as if they were inferior.

Additionally, I can recall my dad and stepmom having to diffuse these issues or sort through this process with us on a consistent basis. I have vivid memories of repeating things we heard or were told and can recall Dad trying to explain, support, and protect us from this even as little kids.

While the adults seemed to have many unresolved issues, as a young kid, I really only remember being loved, supported, and taken care of by both of my parents. I remember going back and forth between the homes and always feeling safe, having fun, and enjoying family time.

What's interesting about how things started to transpire as an early teen between my stepdad and me is that the experience was actually the complete opposite for me as a young child. I recall Christmases shortly after my mom remarried when my sister and I were spoiled beyond belief. The tree overflowed with presents, and I felt an immense amount of love and gratitude to be together. We all used to cook together, sing songs at the piano as a family, and fill the house with contagious laughter.

From preschool through elementary school, the holidays, especially Christmas, were only filled with happiness. I also have clear memories of all of my parents at my clarinet concerts, soccer games, track meets, and dance recitals. My stepdad coached girls' soccer in years past, and I can still remember how I felt when he would run up and down the sidelines, cheering me on as if I was the only one on the field. I felt adored, like I could do no wrong, and that someone would always be there for me. Despite all of that, something changed in middle school, and I couldn't help but start to wonder why or what was wrong with me.

As the older sister, Rachael remembers things differently. She shared stories of when our stepdad moved in, how Mom changed, and ultimately, what that felt like. The type of understanding was, "It's his house, so he makes the rules." I remembered things more pleasantly in my childhood until the family fights began in middle school.

Rachael's perspective helped me understand that the change was not as sudden and abrupt as it felt in my preteen years. In hindsight, I believe the controlling and manipulative parenting was happening for many years, and the frustration was building, but it wasn't until I was old enough to stand up for myself, or my sister, that my world started imploding.

As I was getting older, able to "see it," or able to defend myself, issues began to arise with my stepdad. During this time I also realized that while my stepdad was very strict with both of us, he didn't antagonize my sister—only me. As a kid, it made me wonder, *Why me? What's wrong with me?*

It was only through my work with Lisa that I realized it was because I was defensive, ready to fight back, and he could get a rise out of me. Rachael avoided confrontation like the plague. She would've done anything to deflect the spotlight on her and avoid any conflict and he knew he couldn't poke or prod at her like he did me.

I truly believe that Rachael was a much more confident person than I was as a young teen, and she couldn't care less what someone said about her. I, on the other hand, was a "Sensitive Sally" deep inside, so anything unkind or antagonizing set my whole head and heart to a declination. Even if I had a tough shell, my confidence was low, my self-esteem was low, so it was very easy for me to take someone's comments personally, and as the truth, while my sister had this ability to dismiss them.

I was so envious of her inner strength and self-confidence and wished that I didn't allow someone else's thoughts to derail me. Very few saw how I really felt. Most saw a pissed off and argumentative teen.

The biggest problem here was that I didn't know how to express my sadness or hurt. Being vulnerable was foreign to me, so instead of showing the pain or opening up about what was upsetting me, often what occurred was my backlash, my fight back. I often lashed out and fought back with my own rage and retaliation. I hijacked my true emotions, which was not a valid communication of how I was *really* feeling, but rather a way I felt safe. It was a mechanism I taught myself to compensate for the confidence I lacked.

I've felt misunderstood for most of my life. The emotions I outwardly expressed were often not at all what I was actually feeling. As a kid on the curb, I wanted to be held, protected, loved, and feel strong enough to tell people why I was so sad. Instead, I was angry, defensive, and put on the world's strongest front that I didn't care. All of the armor in the world paled in comparison to the shield I built around my heart.

I've always known that I don't just get mad without a reason, but it wasn't until my early 30s when I recognized my triggers. That gave me the ability to articulate what was setting me off and to explain to others how I was feeling and why I reacted in the manner that I did. I finally knew what ignited my fuse to snap or shut down any time I felt violated, manipulated, or needed to self-protect.

As this story unravels, you will see how I avoided my feelings or ran from situations for so long because I couldn't clearly articulate how I felt. I fed the lie that no one would even care, so what was the point of trying? I also fed the lie that even if they cared, they wouldn't understand, so why bother?

It wasn't until college when I finally decided to face things head on. I knew in my heart that I had buried my emotions and feelings for more than a decade. If I didn't want to continue with the anxiety, anger management, and loneliness I was experiencing, I was going to have to address them. Personal development doesn't happen overnight, and in my opinion, it never actually stops if you want to keep growing. Over the years, I slowly started understanding the origin of my defense mechanisms, short temper, and quick-to-react personality.

Between dozens of therapy sessions, hours of journaling, and writing unsent letters to articulate my feelings, I started realizing that many of my childhood memories were triggers for me as an adult. These were the memories seared in my mind of being alone, not being supported, not having someone in my corner, and recalling my family's role in all of it. Many times growing up, my mom tried to avoid conflict or notoriously "didn't want to be in the middle" between her daughter and husband. She would literally say something along the lines of, "That's between you and Pops; I am staying out of it," or "Lauren, it's in the past. Sweep it under the carpet and let's just move on. Why are you still making a big deal out of this?" How can a young girl express her feelings if they are going to be dismissed or overlooked anyway?

Grounded

I had been grounded, (for what this time I'm not sure), and I lost my phone privileges. I came home from middle school and really wanted to wish my good friend a happy birthday. My stepdad had been traveling for work, but I asked my mom if I could use the phone just to leave my friend a message to say happy birthday. Mom said that I could, *if* I made the call in front of her, *if* I only wished her a happy birthday, and *if* I hung up right after. I agreed to the negotiation. My friend did not answer when I called, but I was excited to leave her a voicemail so she knew I was thinking of her.

A couple of hours later we were sitting at our dining room table having dinner. We often had quite formal dinners, even on the weeknights. If my stepdad was not traveling, we sat at the table and always had multiple courses. It was a very timely event. We were not the kids who ate at the counter and ran back to our activities.

The phone rang in the middle of dinner, and it was an absolute no-no to ever answer while we were at the dinner table. If you remember all the way back to the early 1990s, then you know you could hear someone leave a message on the machine. That's what happened next. My friend was returning my call and thanked me for the birthday wishes. My stepdad, who returned home earlier that evening from his trip, started inquiring about why I made a phone call and reiterated that I was grounded and had zero phone privileges.

In the midst of his Hulk-type outburst, I was trying to be heard, explaining that Mom had given me permission, that she saw me leave a message, and that was the only thing I did. My stepdad looked right at her and asked, "Did you give her permission to make the call?" Mom looked right at him, never even making eye contact with me, and said, "No, I did not."

When I look back, the lingering hurt wasn't over a birthday phone message, but rather how sad it made me, how embarrassed I felt, and ultimately, how unprotected I was. I asked myself so many times whether Mom made the choices she did because she was avoiding conflict, if she feared the repercussions of *allowing* me to do something against the rules, or if she simply didn't care about the consequences for me.

This specific memory is a moment I will never forget, simply because, in my eyes at the time, she chose him over me and there was nothing I could do about it. I was so sad, angry, and frustrated. I felt so helpless and kept thinking, *Why should I do the right thing if it doesn't even matter? Whether you are in the right or in the wrong, you're always going to be treated the same way.*

Now, I want to be clear: my mom was absolutely loving, nurturing (especially when we were sick), involved in our childhood activities, and was the Girl Scout troop Mom. When it came to Rachael and me arguing, she didn't intervene. When it came to her husband bullying me, calling me names, or making fun of me, she always looked the other way. I never felt she agreed with how he treated me, it just seemed easier for her not to get involved.

I think that was her way of protecting herself, and surely she knew she was avoiding upsetting him. My mom is the epitome of a peacemaker, only wants to make others happy, and will do whatever it takes to stay far away from confrontation.

As an adult, I can decipher these behavior patterns, but as a child, I remember hurting, being so disappointed, and wondering, *Why isn't Mom sticking up for me?* I created a story in my mind starting in the fifth grade that replayed in my head for decades. The story, the chatter between my ears was, *If Mom wasn't going to stick up for me or defend me, then who will? If my mom didn't love me enough to put me first, then no one would ever love me enough to put me first.*

I started going through life doing whatever I wanted to do. I didn't rely on others because I didn't trust they would be there. I was nearly 10 years old when I first started to safeguard or self-protect. At a very young age, I adopted the defense mechanism of fight or flight that crippled me for the next few decades. I was skeptical, guarded, and at a moment's notice, was ready to attack or ready to run.

Forgiveness

I truly believe that part of living your ideal life and doing personal growth is letting go of past mistakes, forgiving those who hurt you, and also forgiving yourself for what you cannot change. Many of us create stories because of our childhood. Many speakers and authors talk about the effects of codependent parents, passive-aggressive parents, and abusive parents.

While my intent is not to teach those individual roles and consequences, I will share my own story about my relationship with my mom. We all have different experiences, but what I know in my heart is the importance of forgiveness. Holding on to past anger and sadness not only steals joy from our lives, but it also absorbs energy from higher vibrating emotions that benefit us and those around us. My relationship with my mom was not always easy, and at times, quite challenging, but I wouldn't change a thing, knowing the woman I am now and also the very special relationship we get to enjoy today.

My mom and I went through some turbulent times when I was in middle school and even part of high school; however, we've always been close. Our relationship is unique, and while it's been shaky a few times, we are unbreakable. At times, I did not understand her, even wanted to *change* her, but that did not change my knowing deep inside how much she loved me. Even when we were at our worst during my pre-teen years, our unconditional connection never wavered.

The summer after eighth grade, I was getting ready to go to band camp. I know what you're thinking: how many teen rebels were playing the clarinet? As far as I knew, only one. Nonetheless, I was headed out for a long weekend. During many times in my life, my sixth sense, my deep intuition, has been triggered. While I have missed the signal many times, I've also had numerous moments when I paid attention, and thankfully, it led me down the right path.

I knew deep in my heart, deep in my mind, and deep in my gut that if I didn't leave my mom and stepdad's house soon, I was headed toward disaster. Not only was I incredibly unhappy, but I was also hanging out with the wrong crowd. While that rebellion helped me escape some of my frustration and pain, I knew that wasn't the path for me. I talked to my dad and stepmom for a while about moving in with them full time, and the answer was always the same. "Lauren, you are always welcome here, but this is a conversation we have to have with your mom. It's not only up to us."

So many times I wanted to talk about it and was hopeful Mom would support me, but I chickened out in having that talk. In my process of wanting to move and stop being hurt, I found myself protecting her and not wanting to hurt her, more than I was looking out for my own best interest; therefore, I did nothing.

I finally got the courage to write a long letter to tell her that I was moving, not because of her, but because of the situation with my stepdad. As she dropped me off at the bus for camp, I gave her the letter. I knew she would have a few days to process it, and I knew I wasn't going to see her sad or mad the next few days. I prayed she would want the best for me and support my request of wanting to live with my dad for good.

When I returned from camp, I felt a lot of guilt, an immense amount of shame, and was definitely ridiculed by my family for leaving a letter and running off to camp. I know it seems like a cop-out to write a note and not have a conversation, but nonverbal communication has always been easier for me, especially as a pre-teen. My mom and stepdad did not necessarily support me, but when I insisted that I would involve the courts and that my dad was ready to do what it took to get me into his house, the decision was made.

My mom and I barely spoke the first couple of months after I moved. Not only were cell phones, text messaging, and social media not around then, but I knew she was incredibly hurt. I was frustrated and hurt with the situation, so I just moved on with a great deal of unresolved emotions, but I felt guilt, shame, and blamed myself for leaving. During the first year I was at my dad's, not only were my mom and I not talking, but we were also not spending any time together.

After months of not seeing her, I decided to go to her house for Christmas. Within hours of being there, history repeated, and I found myself back outside, on the curb, crying, waiting for my dad to race down from Boulder to come get me. I remember thinking, *What was the point? Why did I even try to come visit?*

Furthermore, it drove an even bigger wedge between us. I was so mad... I had been away for months, and when I came back, I found myself in the same situation of my stepdad pushing my buttons, me snapping, and ultimately, getting kicked out. It was so hard to just sit back and watch and utter her famous words, "That's between the two of you. I am staying out of it."

Sometimes I wonder if maybe my mom thought I was so strong that she didn't think I would be negatively affected by stepdad's taunting, so she chose to look the other way, but in all honesty, I think she didn't want to let him down and didn't want to upset him, and she knew I would love her unconditionally.

Over the years we have become incredibly close again, but a lot of tough conversations and forgiveness happened to help us heal together. One pivotal moment ignited both of our hearts and provided an unspoken but immense amount of forgiveness.

My Nana was my dad's mom, but she and my mom were always very close even after my parents' divorce. They talked on the phone regularly and had weekly luncheons. My Nana had emphysema and became very sick, ultimately ending up in hospice. Of all my relatives, aunts, uncles, cousins—anyone—my Nana was always my favorite. She was the one who always protected me, babied me (maybe because I am the youngest of all of her grandkids), and most importantly, understood me.

I always knew Nana saw my huge heart through my thick shell. During her final days, I spent a significant amount of time at the hospice center about an hour away from my dad's house and five minutes from my mom's house. Instead of going back and forth to Boulder each day, I chose to stay with my mom so I could be closer for more visits.

The night Nana passed it had been just my mom and me at the hospice center for a few hours. I remember us sitting on each side of the bed, and while we each held Nana's hands resting across her stomach, my mom and I were holding hands, too. We left that night and said goodbye, both knowing this was the last time we'd ever see Nana. My uncle called a few hours later to let us know Nana had passed.

My mom and I have never spoken about that week, especially that night, and how it brought us back together, but it was an unspoken understanding of love, time, and family we both felt. Innately, I think we both forgave each other for the hurt we had caused. I believe we both knew how much we loved each other, and conclusively, knew that even if I wasn't living with her, or even if we handled conflict differently, our relationship would always be special.

Shortly after my Nana passed, my mom and I recognized our special bond. We did better at spending time together one-on-one rather than with the rest of the family. We had many unresolved issues with my stepdad, however, neither of us wanted to miss out on our mother-daughter moments.

Unfortunately, we didn't spend much time together during the remainder of my high school years. I rarely went back to her house, and she seldom drove to see me. Once I had my driver's license and a car, we used to meet in the middle for lunches. During these times, my relationship with my mom started changing. It's not that I didn't respect her or see her as a parental figure, but since I wasn't living with her, we started to become more like friends.

I found her so easy to talk to, so relatable in certain ways, and began to see a level of compassion, support, and empathy that I craved in my life. Our lunch dates evolved into girls' weekends when she came to visit me in college. She would come up and stay with me, and I can just remember laughing hysterically and spending the best of times together. Whether we were prepping meals or watching old movies, she was so easy to be around, to talk to. I started to really notice how *proud* she was of me.

The interesting part was we never spoke about my stepdad or any of the past issues. We simply "brushed them under the carpet" and enjoyed our present time together. When I moved to Arizona for graduate school, our relationship became closer and we continued our girls' trips. My mom came down to visit me many times and I absolutely loved our weekends together. It was during this time that I was also beginning my fitness career, which accelerated my personal growth journey.

Over the years, my personality softened, but if I am being honest, I was just as temperamental. A few times I came home from Arizona when the entire family got together. That was how I established the relationship I have with my stepdad that still exists today. We have a mutual respect and love for my mom and learned how to "play nice."

When the family gets together, regardless of the location, he and I are cordial to one another, polite, but have little to no interaction. It is interesting because I know how much he cares about me, and how much gratitude I have for everything that shaped me to be the woman I am today; however, I think the inability to communicate about the past deeply hinders what could be possible today.

Over the years, I have asked my mom a bit about my childhood and how she felt. Tough conversations aren't that enjoyable for many people, including my mom. She often told me, "Lauren, let it go. Why are we worried about the past?" "Lauren, that was so long ago. Let's just focus on today." While I am grateful for the positivity, it's a challenge for me to not get closure and process through past struggles.

I've never asked my stepdad about why he did or said what he did, and I can't recall ever hearing an apology. For months, years, even decades, I prayed and wished he would just say he was sorry, but it hasn't happened yet. Part of my forgiveness journey was not only releasing the desire for an outcome that doesn't look like it will ever happen, but also doing my best to understand the situation from his perspective and hers, and not only seeing the memories through my lens.

My mom now sends me daily texts, weekly cards, and truly is in my corner to the umpteenth degree. When she first started to "show up" in my life this way, I resented her. I remember thinking, *Why now? Where were you then?* That resentment could be turned on or off like a light switch, and I knew I could make the choice to focus on what I cannot change from the past or I could focus on the present and be grateful for what's happening now. So many people would love a mom like I have today. It was easier for me to focus on the present, where we were going, and not allow the past to hold us back.

Ever since I went to college, she has been my rock, cheerleader, friend, and encourager. While things will never be perfect, and the past cannot be undone, we grew closer, forgave one another, and now enjoy a very loving, respectful relationship as adults. Some traits and characteristics I do not wish to acquire, such as the inability to address conflict, and I respect our differences, but I see many other traits in her that I only hope to embody.

Why am I telling you all of this? As I said, it's important for you to understand what transpired, how I created my shell, and how it haunted me until I cracked the code many years later. Who I am today, the voice I have for others, and the impact I want to make for those who suffer in silence didn't always exist. Years of trauma, fear, and anxiety, followed by years of personal development, growth, coaching, and therapy allows me to share. My experience empowers me to piece the puzzle of life together, to understand how and why I became so guarded, distrusting, and easily triggered.

Most importantly, it opened my eyes and heart to let go of the past, be vulnerable, and ultimately, trust again. This allows me to be a leader, influencer, and catalyst for change in others. Forgiveness and healing were the first steps to helping me get off the curb.

FROM BULLIED TO BULLY

"Your earrings are so big even birds could perch on them."

"Think your hair could be slicked back any tighter, Dooners?" (An awful nickname my stepdad gave me referring to the Lorna Doone cookie.)

"Got your Marlboros with you, Lauren? Don't forget your smokes."

"Don't forget you're white, Lauren. I know you seem confused these days, but you're not actually an African-American."

"Are you having another racial identity crisis?"

These were a few of the daily comments I heard on my way to school, specifically middle school. My sister Rachael and I had rooms in the basement, and I used to dread climbing the flight of stairs that led to the rest of the house. I knew that as soon as I opened the door and into the kitchen that smelled like Folgers coffee and men's aftershave, I was stepping into the target zone, and the comments would begin.

I felt like the coffee wasn't the only thing brewing in the morning; my stepdad was also brewing with remarks and crude comments ready to incite me. I remember setting my alarm so early and taking pride in getting ready. I wanted to be fashionable and well-presented... only to get in the car and be ripped apart, from my hair to my jewelry, jeans, perfume, you name it. No matter what I did, deep down I always felt it wasn't good enough or something was wrong with me.

This was an ongoing event that made my stomach churn and my heart hurt. My stepdad often dropped my sister and me off to school on his way to work, or he would be drinking coffee while we were eating breakfast at the counter, so no matter what, we had no escape. I wanted to believe deep down that he cared about me and simply had a terrible sense of humor, but the truth was I felt so small, never enough, that all of my flaws were on the forefront, and all of my attributes buried under the ridicule.

I remember countless days getting out of the car so pissed off because I had just been taunted, teased, and degraded for the last 10-15 minutes. Seriously, who starts their day that way? If adolescence and middle school weren't hard enough (from your peers and your own hormonal struggles), my mom's home didn't even feel protected. My own family made me feel so small, so insignificant.

I was embarrassed to bring friends over after school or on the weekends, knowing I was going to be mocked and insulted, and no one in my family was going to stand up for me. I can recall always feeling so ashamed going to class, feeling so insecure, never good enough, and on the verge of tears. Unfortunately, I also was too proud to let anyone know how I was really feeling.

When it came to my classmates, I was too tough to show the incredible ache inside. I didn't want anyone to think I was weak, so I never shared this sadness, never opened up about what was eating me up inside. Instead, I put up a massive front to mask what was really going on. I felt in control, or *strong*, when I got angry and adopted an "I don't give a f**k" attitude in order to cope with how much I was hurting and how ashamed I felt. In addition to burying the *truth* behind these feelings, sadly, I also coped by projecting what was happening to me onto others.

Unfortunately, and wistfully, at that time in my life, the only way I thought I could make myself feel better was by bringing down others. I found popularity, or so I thought, through being a bully, which reinforced this terrible behavior. I was taught, or it was exemplified (over and over) that it was OK to make fun of people, and regrettably, I got good at doing it to others. It made sense because that was the shame-filled culture I was experiencing day in and day out.

Today, I wish I could go back and apologize to so many kids and tell them I am sorry for hurting them. There is no justification, no excuse, but now that I understand why I did what I did, I simply wish I could apologize to anyone I ever hurt. It breaks my heart knowing I made others cry and shook their confidence.

It saddens me that I intimidated other children or disrupted their childhood as a result of my poor coping skills. I didn't realize at the time, but I thought I was finding my strength by finding the flaws in others. Simultaneously, I justified my hurtfulness simply because it made me feel less isolated. I wasn't the only broken one, right? I wasn't the only one with a messed-up life, right?

A major consequence of these choices was that I fueled the isolation I was already experiencing. Not only was I lacking the warm fuzzies at home, but I didn't really have any true friends. I had a lot of acquaintances who were trying to stay on my good side out of fear, but not very many people close to me. I had no one I could confide in—nobody who was there for me without judgment.

The combination of my guarded heart and my bully of a personality prevented the close bonds in which I could open up, talk, and gain the benefits of true friendship. I was never afraid, just sad, and constantly wanting an *out* of feeling the way I did. No one wanted to be friends with the bully, and if they were my friend, most were because they were scared of me, and not because they genuinely cared about me.

The feeling I had on the curb on Christmas, of being all alone, started showing up in the classroom, in the lunchroom, and on field trips. I didn't know it then, but I understand now, that in the process of trying to protect or defend myself, I was literally pushing everyone else away.

In addition to being a mean girl, I also stopped caring. I stopped caring what others thought. I stopped caring what would happen to me. I stopped caring who I hurt along the way. I remember adopting an "I don't give a shit" attitude, which led me into worse decisions.

I was carrying so much heartache, so much loneliness, and so much anger around inside, the only way I knew to escape it was acting out. I found myself using drugs and alcohol at a young age. How many 11 and 12-year-olds do you know who are getting drunk on the weekends, ditching class to smoke cigarettes, and getting high on a daily basis? Whether it was marijuana, glue, Ritalin, or alcohol, I quickly found ways to numb the pain.

I never made attempts to kill myself because I was too afraid of failing (being unsuccessful at the attempt) and then I would be in even more trouble, but that didn't keep me from having morbid thoughts (on and off) for many of my pre-teen and early teen years. I used to wonder if people would miss me if something happened to me.

I used to wonder, *Would everyone's life be better if Lauren wasn't around?* Most kids fear getting in trouble, and I would ponder what trouble I could get into that would be bad enough I would end up in juvenile hall, which at the time seemed better than my current situation. I recognize how premature this thinking was, but recall having a feeling that maybe I would *belong* there, since everywhere else I was feeling out of place.

Some nights I would just lie in my bed and wonder what heaven was like. It had to be better than this hell of a lonely, isolated place I was experiencing then. I remember asking the question, "Would anyone miss me?" I knew I was loved, especially by extended relatives and family on my dad's side, but the emptiness in my heart invited a dark cloud to cover up my true self, my dreams, goals, and what I *really* wanted life to be. I was trapped in sadness, pain, and loneliness.

I found myself physically fighting in middle school simply because I didn't know how to handle the frustration inside. For years, especially as a young teen, I felt like a shaken two-liter pop bottle, ready to explode, and embarrassingly so, that's often exactly what occurred. So much emotion was stuffed inside that someone could look at me the wrong way, or God forbid, they actually say something snarky, and I was ready to unleash. Inappropriately and deplorably, I often did. I also found myself doing anything to get attention about what was happening. I hoped that if enough people saw my rebellions, it would be my ticket out of *that* house.

I was intentionally acting out, praying someone would see what a day in my life was like. I was deliberately rebelling, begging for anyone to notice how I felt inside and not just see what I was representing on the outside. Physical abuse is often obvious to others, and is what we think of when we hear the word abuse, but emotional torment is hidden, often not necessarily seen by others. The popular adage I heard as a kid went: "Sticks and stones may break my bones, but names will never hurt me," and every time I heard it, I thought that's not true, the names are what hurt the most!

Since the consequences of emotional affliction are not easily visible, it's common for those who have been violated or victimized to hold their hurt inside because of the shame and blame they experience. More often than not, instead of getting *rescued*, I wounded up grounded, which further perpetuated this feeling of isolation and loneliness. I remember just sitting in my room, with no TV, no phone, no friends, and being far away from my dad's house. Even though I was in my basement bedroom, the feeling was no different from sitting outside on the curb. I was left to stir my thoughts and fuel the fire of frustration inside of me.

My feelings may have been immature (I was only a pre-teen and early teen), but this was my reality, my day-to-day hell through middle school. I was too embarrassed to tell people that I was getting picked on by an adult. Everyone would just see my brokenness, right? I was too embarrassed to tell people my mom didn't stick up for me.

I was too afraid of others seeing what my stepdad saw in me, so I never really opened up to anyone except my dad and stepmom. As a result, I became a professional at masking all of the anguish with anger, defensiveness, and ultimately found my kryptonite and expert representation of self-protection: fight or flight.

I will never claim to be an angel child, and many would argue I was actually quite the opposite, a problem child; however, as I got older and gained greater clarity around the behavior and patterns I exemplified, I started understanding why I was so off the beaten path. I recognized what led me to make such poor decisions and ultimately why my emotions were so mistaken by others.

Champions in Your Corner

Sometimes we can see in others what they don't yet see in themselves, and sometimes people can see in us what we don't yet see in ourselves. Even without saying what's going on, often people can intuitively tell something's wrong. The heroes you want, the champions in your corner, will know what level of love you need, find a way to be there, and provide support. These individuals are the ones who see through the masks and get right to your core. During these incredibly challenging middle school years, two instrumental women believed in me. They shone their light in my life so brightly I knew whatever I was experiencing was going to be temporary.

The first lady was my eighth-grade teacher Miss Vail. She had a special way of making me feel seen when I didn't feel seen or heard at all. She also had a way of encouraging me, believing me, and guiding me to stay on track, even when I was so checked out. I can recall her pouring greatness into me during detention after school. I remember her seeing my strengths, edifying me, and making me feel special.

Miss Vail cast a vision that this time in my life was temporary, that I had my whole life ahead of me, and to stay focused on what would come, not just on what was. She made it a point for me to see that the choices I was making would hurt *me* the most, especially in the long run, if I didn't clean up my act. When I look back, I had a sense of her having my back, even though I never *really* shared with her how I felt. The coolest part was that she gave me hope and belief in myself. She believed in me enough that I started getting proactive about changing the situation. It was Miss Vail who gave me the strength to move out of my mom's house and into my dad's.

The second incredible influence and shining light in my life was my Aunt Patti, my dad's brother's wife. After the whole family was together for a Jewish family dinner, one in which I was mouthing off and ruining the evening for everyone, I remember Aunt Patti taking me outside to talk. She told me a story about champions and explained that we all have champions in our life, but they are limited, rare, and special. Once you exhaust your champions, they don't usually return.

Aunt Patti explained to me that I needed to get it together because while she empathized with what I was experiencing, she did not give permission for me to treat innocent peers a certain way. She didn't condone my poor behavior at school, and she certainly wasn't going to tolerate the disrespect I was showing to the side of the family that was in my corner, supporting me, and that was not to blame for my torment and bitterness.

Aunt Patti was always someone I loved and respected. She was so level-headed, with a laugh that could elevate anyone or any room at any given time. I'm not confident I would've received or responded to that advice in the same way if it came from someone else; however, because I loved and adored her so much, and I could tell she truly wanted to help me, not just punish or lecture me, so I didn't react with my typical averting, "I don't give a shit" teen rebellion.

Instead, I started believing people were in my corner with my best interests at heart. It was only a 5- to-10-minute conversation, but it still stands out to me today. Her message was pivotal. It shook me to my core and awakened my heart to love when it had been so jaded from the other disenchanting relationships in my life at that time. In fact, her words of wisdom revived me, and for the first time, instead of focusing on the anguish and frustration, I started feeling gratitude for the family that wanted the best for me, for the few true friends I had, and ultimately for the ability to make a choice.

I'm immensely grateful for those two true champions from that season of my life, but I also think of the special people in my life I am a champion for today. For just a moment, think about someone in your history who guided or influenced you to the point your life looks completely different today because of that person. Give them a call. Send them a note. Share what they said or did that made such a profound effect on who you are today. Imagine if they hadn't done what they did for you.

Think about who you've been a champion for in their life. When I think about where I volunteer now, how I lead my business, or even the first career path I took into criminal justice, so much of it has to do with one middle school teacher who believed in me. It was one chat in the driveway with my Aunt Patti that made me feel again. That was when I started to feel the shift away from being the bully and breaking down others to becoming the champion fighting for those who need to know they matter and empowering people wherever they are.

Each of us could use another person in our corner of the ring in life. What I didn't know at the time was that I was already in a fight for my life, not to survive but to thrive!

Fight or Flight

It wasn't until much later on in life I realized I mastered the chaos of fight or flight. Looking back now, I spent nearly three decades in fight or flight mode whenever I was triggered. I was ready to go toe-to-toe with a physical or verbal fight, and could fight with the best of them. When I felt violated, out of control, unsafe, or vulnerable, I would run away, (sometimes literally), or completely shut down. In other words, if I couldn't defend myself, I would dodge it, and if I had nowhere to go, then I would just guard up, ignite my shield, and shut out whatever was happening, emotionally and communicatively.

I was a master of saying, "It's fine," or, "Never mind," or, "I'm fine," when I felt I couldn't handle the situation or might get hurt. I was also a professional at escaping a situation. If I wasn't around, it couldn't hurt me, right? I could guard up and get into battles with anyone since I convinced myself the way to avoid pain was to shift sadness into anger and fight back harder, and if this wasn't an option, I would take off. Running away was always my plan B.

This coping mechanism showed up in my life for years at work, with friends, with family, and in so many other ways. Many of my relationships suffered, as well as my own emotional intelligence because I could sense a feeling of mistrust, a sense of being violated, manipulated, or being deceived, and with the drop of a hat I would snap or shut down. I hadn't learned effective communication or how to express emotion, which meant I often retaliated or escaped.

Time and time again, I found myself in a familiar situation or one that resembled the same emotion of *sitting on the curb* after fights with my sister, bad dates, family issues, work conflicts, and the list goes on. Even today, it is a conscious decision to take time to carefully respond without allowing my subconscious mind to switch into a flight or fight reaction. I will have triggers that could set me off, but I choose to believe it's not intentional, that people are good, that people are not trying to hurt me, and therefore, I am not so quick to react defensively.

I choose to communicate in ways where I am seen, heard, and respected, the same way I see, hear, and respect others. It's a decision to respond thoughtfully and not react immediately. While it is innate for me to react and not respond, I know firsthand that doesn't serve me or anyone else, and consciously choose to behave differently today. For so many, including myself, it requires daily practice and reinforcement to change conditioned behaviors from something we are used to into something we actually want and choose.

Core Shame—Not Good Enough

Have you ever known someone who always seemed out of control because they are busy trying to control everything they *can't* control? That was a phrase I heard from a business coach many years ago, but it resonated with me. I was that person. Correction: I often still am that person. We've all heard the phrase "let go," but I think we can all agree that is much easier said than done.

I was the gal so worried about other people's decisions or outcomes beyond my reach that I was unsettled, frustrated, or stressed. Additionally, I often felt anxiety over making sure everything always went just right. I worked myself into a frenzy obsessing over unnecessary details or impossible perfection. If I was getting ready with a friend, I would get so uneasy and hot-tempered if we were running late. I got so uptight worrying about disrespecting other people's time and what judgments they would make if we were late. I'm quite confident that friend didn't even want to go out with me anymore.

When I planned group dinners for my company, I cared so much about being respectful of the restaurant's time and the other guests' times that, when people showed up late, it frustrated me, and *everyone* knew, as opposed to just letting the disappointment go and moving on. The negative energy I allowed to exude from me in those situations was so intense others could definitely feel it.

I think we all want to be liked, but it is impossible to please everyone. As a group fitness instructor, I want to be prepared, and of course I want to make sure my members have a great experience; however, not everyone is going to like my music selection, or not everyone wants the room the same temperature, and the worry about my class being good enough (translation: *Am I good enough?*) would steal my joy and love for teaching group fitness. How could I possibly control everyone else's experience? It was so much pressure focusing on others' behavior that everyday life wasn't fun anymore for me or anyone around me.

It's a weird feeling to take ownership, to feel responsible for the experience of others, but so often I apply that pressure, which leaves those around me wondering, "What's wrong with Lauren?" "What's Lauren so stressed about?" I have faint memories of my parents, specifically my dad, behaving in the same type of way. This is another area where I felt misunderstood, so often I felt others were interpreting my behavior as controlling or bossy, when in actuality, I just wanted to provide the best experience and be respectful of everyone involved.

Like most people, I think some personality traits are genetic, but I also believe many are learned. Nature versus nurture, right? When I think about my dad, the apple didn't fall far from the tree. He is the epitome of taking on responsibility, making sure everything is just right, and much like his baby girl, a bit of a *worry wart*. As kids, my sister and I would joke and tell him to take a "chill pill," or to be as "mellow as a yellow cello," but he often was very stressed, high strung, and wound up. In retrospect, much of this angst was over things out of his control, not his responsibility, but his pride and dedication permitted this disarray.

As a teen and young adult, I can recall times when I could sense my dad's tension or frustration, but I was also old enough or mature enough to know that he wasn't upset with anyone. He simply had so much passion and integrity for what he was doing that he allowed himself to get worked up. I look back now and can laugh as I think how stressful Passover dinners could be, and then I think about my own Friendsgivings—they're much the same. Whether it was major events for his company conference or attending a family function, his attention to detail never went unnoticed. So often in my life, I obsess over each detail or want everything to go better than planned that I literally take the fun out of it. Clearly, people don't want to be around a stress ball, even if your intentions are good.

People sense it when I'm coming across as a "fun sponge," and I know this is an area I've been misunderstood. While I was working *so hard* to please others, to fulfill my "I am not good enough" story or provide an exceptional experience, it often left others feeling like they disappointed me, or were afraid they would.

It wasn't until I coached with Lisa that I first understood and recognized the behavior and then I was able to relax and accept what I couldn't control, and do the best for what I could control. While in the process of doing the best I could, I could also be vulnerable and actually share the emotion I was feeling so others could empathize and not feel defensive or at fault by my current state of overwhelm.

*****

I remember riding in the car from Denver to Boulder, the commute between my parents' homes, always in the back seat. Rachael used to get car sick so she got to sit up front. Indirectly, she was more easily heard, and while I was in the back, I can still recall wondering if anyone really understood me, knew what I was feeling, or questioned why I was so guarded, so defensive, so short-fused. It's not that every time we got in the car we weren't chatting or I was ignored; however, sometimes during traffic, bad weather, or when I was tired, it was where I found solitude and time to process through emotions... specifically during the middle school years.

I remember thinking that Rachael had it so easy. Not only was she skinny (I was 'thick'), but she was smart, followed the rules perfectly, and was never picked on or bullied. As a child, it was too complex for me to understand why I was the target. Subconsciously, I created a story of not being loved, not being worthy, not being enough, and so forth, instead of taking ownership of or acknowledging our personality differences.

Rachael so easily shared her good grades and everything wonderful with her extracurricular activities, but I wanted to be invisible, as I had to discuss what "issues" I had or explain the poor choices I had been making. Today, I understand that my personality and Rachael's are dynamically different. The reaction people could provoke out of me is something no one would've ever been able to get out of her.

When I did personality testing with my life coach, I was finally able to clarify why I behaved a certain way and why my reactions were so monumentally different from my sister's. It's also interesting to look back with gratitude to see how those experiences set me up for who I am today. Part of why Rachael and I are still as different as we've ever been is because of how our childhood experiences shaped us.

Boundaries

Part of my not good enough story is my fear of disappointing others. I am not a people pleaser in that I am fake or adjust to make others happy, nor am I overly concerned about others' opinions of me; however, I don't ever want to let someone down or hurt someone's feelings. Sometimes I joke that the downside of being popular is how easy it is to overcommit and over obligate, but truthfully, it's difficult to want to say yes to everything but not be able to.

The minute I want to say no my stomach churns with the fear I have disappointed someone. More often than not, I want to say yes, but with limited hours in the day and a growing entrepreneur's schedule, it is absolutely impossible to say yes to every lunch invite, every coffee appointment, every happy hour, every party, and so forth.

For so long I struggled with trying to say yes to it all because that was my only way of expressing I was good enough. Today I know, because of my internal confidence, that I am a great friend, a loving daughter, a supportive sister, and an incredible partner, but to be all of those things, I needed to learn how to manage my time and let go of the fear that people expected me to commit to everything.

I needed to learn how to set boundaries. Have you ever wanted to just have a chill night in but committed to a dinner party you didn't really want to attend? Have you ever felt like your to-do list is getting brushed aside because of everything you volunteered to do or offered to help with? It's a fine line between putting in the effort and making time for what matters but also giving yourself permission to not do it all.

You can't pour from an empty cup. I used to feel guilty if I ever did anything for myself, as I felt I needed to be doing something for somebody else, but what I've learned is the more I take care of me, the more I can serve and give to others. Whether this means getting in a hot yoga class or enjoying some retail therapy, the more I fuel my soul the more I can fuel others.

What are the areas in your life that drain you that you wish you weren't doing? What are the things you love to do, that if time and money were of no issue you would be doing more of? How can you daily, weekly, monthly, take time to take care of you and simultaneously learn to exercise your 'no' muscle when needed?

In addition to feeling overly independent, I also wanted to be overly in control. I shared with you how my inner child often felt buried. My fear of what others think has held me back from living more freely, but I am surely grateful when I break free. One of the most impactful and life-shifting moments was when I traveled in New Zealand, a story that I share later on, but until then, and often still today, I allow control to dictate my free spirit. I still sometimes struggle with suffocating the playful moments with my seriousness, rigidness, and wanting everything to be just right, but I'm learning how to play well with others. It seems silly to say now, but I think we all sometimes forget what it's like to play and enjoy what makes life so vivid and important.

Free to Play

For the past 20 to 25 years, I've heard many comments such as "Let go," "Relax," "You're so uptight," and "Loosen up, Laur!" While I'm confident I know how to have a good time, especially if I have a glass or two of wine, I'm also someone who likes to be in control, like being good at things, and is highly competitive, which often gets in the way of just being. Somewhere as an early teen I lost my inner child... the fun, carefree, and bountiful soul who lives in the moment, doesn't have a worry in her heart and is full of playfulness.

I believe it was a result of self-protection, combined with fear and mistrust, because during the years kids were playing and being positively supported, I was being taunted. I rebelled and missed out on those playful moments. Additionally, I endured some incredible trauma at the end of high school that perpetuated this ability to feel free, carefree, and in the moment.

Over the years, as a young adult, and as an adult, I've wanted to play so many times, but I got too nervous about what I would look like or what others would think. I can think of times I wanted to play on the swings at a park, dance at a wedding, or even participate in recreational team sports, but the fear of judgment (even from myself) held me back. We've all heard the saying, "moments that take your breath away," and when I think of times that I was just in the moment, a real-life, grown-up kid, feeling happy, or knowing I was good enough, one particular memory always comes to mind.

Ryan (the man I love with my whole heart and the love of my life) and I were walking out of the grocery store one evening, and I was freezing. We had gone out for a fun midnight snack, and it was so cold. I tried to get him to run to the car with me, as walking was taking too long and surely not warming me up, but my attempt to drag him and run with me wasn't exactly successful.

To my surprise, and what felt out of nowhere, he laughed and said, "Are you really doing this right now?" and I replied, "Yes, it's cold!" He said, "Why don't we skip?" Without any hesitation, I grabbed his hand and we skipped through the parking lot. In a matter of seconds, I was giddy, giggly, goofy, and happy.

I couldn't remember the last time I was so present, in the moment, and unconcerned about what anybody thought. To some people this may seem minuscule, but for me, the mid-30-year-old, uptight and overcontrolling perfectionist, it was liberating not to be judged, to be present, and to play!

Sometimes, when we least expect it, we find our goofiness, and a wholesome power to simply *being*. Simply soaking up life and loving those moments is what makes us breathe deeper and know we don't have to live under so much pressure to be perfect.

We've all heard the saying, "laugh like no one is listening and dance like no one is watching," but it's true! Imagine if we could all just *be*... without the reservations of the opinions of others.

NO LONGER MISUNDERSTOOD

You're probably noticing a trend in this book where I always felt *mistaken*. No matter what I said or how I acted, I couldn't get across what I was actually thinking or feeling. My body language and my actions were a misrepresentation of who I truly was and the perception was so different from who I really am.

I used to hear things such as, "Why is Lauren so angry?" "What's wrong with Lauren?" "Wow, you're friends with Lauren?! She is so intimidating." These were sayings I often heard as a kid, teenager, and young adult, and if I'm not careful how I communicate or carry myself, they can still show up today.

Enough Is Enough—The Catalyst for Change

I was at a charity event with a friend when I finally hit the *enough is enough* point. A guy I had been dating had lied to me... again. Earlier in the week I invited him to the event, and he responded that he had to work. The night of the event he confirmed he was staying in.

When my girlfriend and I walked into the venue, not only was this man there, but he made direct eye contact with me, then completely ignored me. While I tried to hold back the tears all evening, not because I had deep feelings for him, but rather because of the feelings of rejection and mistrust. Have you ever felt the way?

I wasn't even that interested, but once again, I felt rejected. Not good enough. Not even good enough to get a man I didn't even like. I struggled to connect with other friends and colleagues that night as the story in my head blasting on repeat kept interfering. *I'll never find anyone. What's wrong with me? Why am I not good enough? You're 34 and still single.* And, *If I was skinnier, he would like me.* As my friend and I drove home that night, I was so annoyed with her because she is gorgeous and thin and had to damn near beat men off with a stick she had so much attention that night. I couldn't hold back the tears anymore.

I remember her telling me, "Lauren, call Lisa Foster." She had been through Lisa's life coaching program and raved about how profound her transformation was after working with Lisa that I was at least open to the consultation. I am a huge believer in the adage, "If something is going to change... something has to change." I had finally reached a threshold where I simply could not handle the feeling of being alone on the curb anymore.

I called Lisa.

After spending countless hours in therapy and thousands of dollars on coaching, I was beyond skeptical about hiring yet another expert. My business was thriving, my physical body was at a place where I was happy and confident, and I had the best girlfriends in the world. While so many pieces of my life puzzle were coming together, a couple of areas were still off.

The first was relationships with my mom and sister, as I still snapped at them or was too quick to jump to conclusions. The second was my romantic relationships with men. I found myself not being clear about what I was looking for in a life partner, but wanting it so badly that I was tolerating being mistreated, picking guys who did not respect me, treat me well or align with my values and dreams. Ultimately, I was not attracting a man who was supportive, compassionate, driven, and so much more. I was settling for men who were dishonest, disrespectful, and selfish—the complete opposite of the ideal man I desired.

If you were to interview Lisa about our first conversation, I suspect she would say, "Lauren was very direct, assertive, and strong-willed." Lisa may also confirm I was full of doubt and skepticism, and fearful of getting *excited* someone could help me only to end up in the same place I started. I was afraid of not making progress or experiencing lasting changes; however, I was willing to do whatever it took to complete these missing puzzle pieces in my life

I felt almost militant as I interviewed Lisa, literally drilling her with questions. Within a matter of minutes, I felt a level of ease come over me like never before. Her kind and light-spoken voice calmed my nerves, but her articulate, confident, and educated demeanor established trust. While she explained her program to me, what it looked like, and what I could expect, I recall having an overwhelming understanding that if I wanted to get better I had to be real, honest, and *vulnerable.*

In the past, with court-ordered therapy or counseling sessions, I didn't want to be there, and simply mastered the game of saying what counselors wanted to hear so I could be done with the obligation. I had too much pride and ego to be real and raw. I *hid* a lot of my truths, a lot of my emotions. As a result, I didn't grow because I was *masking* what was really going on.

Even before I met Lisa in person, I knew she was not judgmental. I was confident she was empathetic and supportive, and I instinctively knew that if I really wanted things to change, I was going to have to be defenseless. For the first time ever, I needed to lay all of my cards on the table, and expose my truths, in order to heal.

I committed to hiring Lisa, and before our first session, she sent me the links to three personality tests: Myers Briggs, StrengthsFinder, and the Enneagram. After sending my results to her I received an email, which was the first step in unraveling this mess of a personality I created and hid behind for years. Her email, which had to do with a conversation we were having around the Enneagram, simply said, "Wow! You are a powerhouse! I can't wait to be in a room with you!!" I remember feeling joyful because I felt like she got me. At the same time, however, I was also slightly offended, thinking, *Powerhouse? What the heck is that supposed to mean?! Is that a polite adjective for intimidating?* As I sat through my first 90-minute appointment, I knew Lisa offered a *safe* place, trusted her expertise, and I was on the road to recovery.

In my first meeting with Lisa, she reviewed my "one sheet," a summary of the three personality test results. I had taken similar assessments in the past, like The Color Code and career surveys, but they never really resonated with me. I actually thought they were quite cheesy and wonky, almost like fortune cookies for business professionals.

On the other hand, Lisa didn't review generic answers; she explained how these characteristics actually show up in life, with work, and relationships, and even self-awareness. I remember for the first time ever thinking these tests were written for me! I usually didn't believe in these types of assessments, considered them vague, or felt my answers could change over time. I never gave them much merit. This time was different, especially when it came to the Enneagram and the Clifton StrengthsFinder.

When I connected with Lisa, I remember having the biggest ah-ha moment of my life. Not only did I have a rapid flashback of so many incidents in my past with clarity about why I did what I did, but also a rapid flash of the future. I saw what I wanted to do and who I could be if I wasn't playing small and started showing up in the world as the best version of me. I will be the first to say I am not an Enneagram or StrengthsFinder expert; however, I want to share some of my biggest takeaways, not only because they were so impactful in my healing journey, but also because I've seen the impact this knowledge and awareness makes on so many others.

Clifton StrengthsFinder has identified 34 strengths in four major areas: strategic thinking, executing, influencing, and relationship building. We all have different strengths, but most of us have four to five prominent strengths.

After taking the test, Lisa educated me on my five strengths: *Achiever, Activator, Significance, Command,* and *Competition.* I will explain each of these a bit more, but it's important to note that none of my strengths are in relationship building or strategic thinking. All of mine are in influencing and executing.

Almost immediately after receiving my test results, I started understanding why I was not naturally empathetic or patient. I've always had a "get shit done" attitude and a "get out of my way; I don't need your permission" personality. As I understood the magnitude and benefits of my strengths, I also understood what Lisa meant by powerhouse personality.

It took only a matter of seconds to look back and understand my decision to graduate from high school early. This decision would feel daunting and overwhelming to most, but for me, it was simple once I made the decision. I understood why people make the faces that they do when I share I have multiple undergraduate and graduate degrees, which doesn't seem unusual or extraordinary to me. I understood why many people can't fathom how much I can accomplish in a day, or why I need to have to-do lists when for me, that is just the way it is.

I finally could explain why I was so impatient, why I put so much pressure on myself, and why people trusted me, knew I would implement a plan, and stand up for the right reason or person. Suddenly, everything was crystal clear for me. I couldn't be a bigger advocate of knowing your strengths, not only to assist you in excelling in areas you are naturally gifted in, and you can empower yourself with, but also to know when to reach out for help in areas where you may not be as talented.

I want to spend a little bit more time on my five strengths: *Achiever, Activator, Significance, Command,* and *Competition.* It's not because my gifts are any greater than anyone else's, but because it has so much to do with the story of how I went from an angry and misunderstood kid to an *activated achiever.*

For the majority of my life, I knew I could always accomplish a lot of things at once, but I didn't understand why everyone else didn't have this ability. On a typical morning, I might be doing two loads of laundry, getting ready, sending emails (thanks to Siri's help), responding to text messages, making the bed, and reviewing choreography for a fitness class, all at the same time.

While this is overwhelming for most, this is how I've always operated.

I know patience isn't innate to me, but to the contrary, when I get an idea, I'm ready to run! The adage is "Ready - aim - fire!" but a friend used to tease me that if I got excited about something, I was "Fire - fire - fire - aim - ready!" because all I want to do is get to work or take action. Over planning and overthinking exhausts me.

Some people want to make sure the plan is flawless before they implement it, while activators like me just dive in, learn, and fix as we go. It's because we feel better actually doing something, not just talking about what we're going to do. I also knew quite early on that people could rely on me.

Whether it was planning a bachelorette party or taking the lead in a school group project, leadership came with ease to me. Peers seemed to respond to my authoritative personality. Some people struggle with where to start, and for me, my struggle has been slowing down. The *activator*, coupled with the proving to be 'good enough,' kept me in a go-go-go way of life.

I also innately knew I didn't want to be like everyone else. That's not intended to be a negative pun, but rather to explain that I resonated with sayings such as "You didn't wake up to be average!" I was willing to go against the grain sometimes to be distinguished. Following the norms wasn't my thing as a child, as a teen, and even now as an adult.

I was annoyed with Lisa, (or maybe myself, but I projected that feeling toward her), when she told me one of my top five strengths (according to StrengthsFinders) was *competitive*. My assumption was that a competitive person wanted to be better than others, when in actuality, it simply means you want to be the best version of yourself and will push the limits to gain growth and to be better than you thought you could be.

One of the areas where I find this to be true is in group fitness classes. I do not show up wanting to be better than everyone; however, if I see someone lifting heavier weights, running faster, or spinning quicker, I have an inner dialogue that says, *If they can do it, I can do it!* I've been in sales and when I see a colleague outperforming me, I am motivated.

To reiterate, this is not to one-up them, but rather to work harder, because *If they can do it... I can do it!* Do you remember when the four-minute mile was unheard of? Once someone ran the first four-minute mile, many others went on to complete the same goal. Sometimes we get in our own way with unleashing our full potential, and watching others exceed what we thought was possible ignites that full potential. That being said, I've embraced this trait and truly try to exceed my upper limit in all areas of life.

Healing Key

Before working with Lisa, at many times I didn't understand myself. Sometimes I recognized a feeling that triggered me to stand up or get out, but I didn't know what triggered me. I knew something was *wrong* when my stomach knotted and my mouth frowned, but even I didn't always recognize what set me off or why my fuse seemed so short. It's fair to say people saw me demonstrate a certain behavior, but the meaning behind my behavior was not clear, even to myself.

It's also accurate to say that I was aware of the disconnect between my emotions and my expressions. It took years, maybe decades, to truly unravel the *causes* behind my eruptions, including why I was so outspoken but inwardly hidden. I never realized how much pain I was covering up or how misinterpreted my body language, words, and energy were until I worked with Lisa. When I began coaching with her, each layer unlocked a greater level of clarity about who I was and why I showed up the way I did, and more excitingly, who I could be and the choices in front of me.

The one-sheet Lisa uses is an aggregation of the three personality tests as part of her life coaching series: The Enneagram, StrengthsFinder, and the Myers-Briggs tests. When Lisa started explaining the Enneagram 8 personality to me, *The Challenger*, I remember feeling for the first time ever that someone truly understood me. The StrengthsFinder results explained my work ethic and daily behaviors, but the Enneagram results were what unlocked the mystery of my multitude of triggers and defensive shell.

Enneagram 8 Self-Protector

Of all of the personality tests in the world, and all of the psychology or sociology assessments or evaluations I've ever done, the Enneagram is the one that forever changed my life. In case you are not familiar with this assessment, I will share some background information with you. I also want to share why this test was so momentous in my life and why I still default to it today for my own personal healing, as well as learning the Enneagram results of others to improve our professional or personal relationships.

The Enneagram number 8, the *challenger*, shows that I have: *desire for control, fear of manipulation or violations, crutch is always be strong and in control, and healing key is to be vulnerable, relax, and let go.*[1]

Lisa started to break down what drives me or what's at the center of all of my decisions: control and safety. She explained to me the different Enneagram personalities and how we all have *healthy expressions* and *unhealthy expressions,* as well as our *healing key.* When we are at our best, when we are confident, and when our driving need is met, we show up as our best selves, our *healthy expressions.*

As a *challenger,* I show up as magnanimous, courageous, decisive, championing, and heroic in my healthy expression. On the other hand, when I am triggered, I feel out of control or the worst yet, violated or manipulated, my *unhealthy expression* shows up as dictatorial, ruthless, megalomaniacal, vengeful, and heartless.

As I read through the list of adjectives of what happens when I am *unhealthy,* I remember a tear rolling down my face. Lisa kindly asked if I was OK and then she asked me a powerful question, *"Lauren, what's coming up for you as you read this?"* I recall feeling a sense of shame or embarrassment that I could behave that way. I knew those pieces of my personality existed; it was everything Rachael referenced when she first told me I was incapable of a healthy relationship. Who would love someone who was heartless and ruthless?

On the other hand, I felt a sense of relief because truly, for the first time ever, I started understanding myself. I was able to forgive myself for behaviors I didn't love or understand about

---

[1] Enneagram Institute

myself, and I was feeling empowered and in control about how to behave differently moving forward.

The final piece was the review of my *healing key*, which is to be vulnerable or to let go. Lisa was explaining to me that when I am feeling out of control or unsafe, the driving emotion of Enneagram 8's, I have a choice. If I don't want to be triggered, then I have to either let go of what I cannot control or be vulnerable by opening up and expressing the discomfort I'm experiencing.

For example, I've always had weird food phobias, so my friends know I am picky about certain restaurants and what I eat. Often, when I was invited to dinner, I immediately got uncomfortable or anxious about what would be served, especially if it was a new restaurant.

If I want to avoid being triggered and see my temperamental, frustrated, edgy and quite challenging (*unhealthy expression*) personality come through, I need to activate my healing key to stay in a *healthy* state. By letting go, I simply surrendered the need to control everything, plan everything, and rationally walk myself through worst-case scenarios.

The second option is to express what I am feeling. "Hey, thank you so much for inviting me to dinner. I am sure my shortness right now is coming across as if I don't want to come and that's not my intention. The restaurant you chose is new to me, and sometimes new places give me a little bit of anxiety, even though it sounds like fun." What seemed so hard for me my entire life suddenly became so clear.

When I first heard about the *challenger* and continued learning more, so many moments of clarity surfaced. If control and safety are most important to me, no wonder it didn't take much for me to fly off the handle. I was also able to see why leadership came naturally to me and how my driving and advocating personality was so impactful to others when I wasn't feeling triggered. I used to always say, "I don't get mad for no reason," and *finally*, I had answers to what provoked the fight or flight reaction. I am not saying that how I handled things was always the best; however, I was relieved to finally make sense of it.

I finally understood why I never settled, why I hit confrontation head-on, and why people naturally trust me. Sometimes when we learn about ourselves, we wish we could change these characteristics, and honestly, it's not always easy to accept. For me, I found the Enneagram 8 to almost be a new level of responsibility.

Whether it be a positive or a negative, taking ownership of an influential personality is simply being aware you have a dramatic effect on others. With the flip of a page, I finally accepted and acknowledged I could be an incredible shaker and mover for others or I could drive people away. I started asking every single day which motivator was controlling my decision-making.

If you can learn a principle or habit, you can also unlearn that same principle or habit. Sometimes it takes longer to break a habit or relearn the modification, but it is possible, with a decision, plan, and focus. I knew right in that moment I could change. I could recognize triggers, and I could make choices about how to express myself. I also knew I had operated a certain way for nearly 34 years. Lasting change doesn't happen overnight, but I was determined to do the work to improve my relationships with others and myself.

People are creatures of habit, and sometimes we don't understand why we do things, even when we are not a fan of what we are doing. Maybe you have noticed how you thrive when you are in a healthy state, or peak place, and on the flip side, you recognize when your ducks are not in a row, similar patterns or behaviors that surface. If I could offer any encouragement or wisdom, I would highly recommend both the Enneagram and StrengthsFinders. Knowledge is power and the first step is having clarity and information to make the changes and amendments you are seeking.

ACTIVATED ACHIEVER: I Am Not A Failure!

Almost Dropout to Activator

The summer before my senior year in high school, I went to register for my classes, and I will never forget when my counselor told me, "Lauren, you are one of the smartest kids in your class, but you aren't going to graduate."

I knew I had been ditching class, and I knew my grades were below average, but I didn't know it was this bad. In my first book, *Why Can't Is A Four Letter Word*, I discuss in detail how I made the decision to graduate early, but simply put, I knew I wanted more than a GED, and I knew I wasn't going to be a high school dropout. Between night school, summer school, and Saturday school, I not only graduated, but I actually graduated a semester early.

A high school diploma might not be important to everyone, but it was extremely important to me. I surely am not the one to place judgment on anyone else's life's decisions, but I wasn't not going to graduate. Completing high school was significant not only because I watched my siblings and many of my friends graduate, and I wanted the same experience, but I also knew the reason I might not graduate was no one's fault but mine. The *I am not a failure* story echoed in my mind. I was going to graduate no matter what because I aspired to do something greater.

I couldn't blame the lack of credits on a health issue or a learning disability. Anyone who knows me knows I am not a quitter, and I was not about to be a high school dropout. I might not always get things right the first time, but my history shows that when it counts, I always turn things around and get things done.

I had started doing drugs at a very early age, but I abruptly stopped that summer before my senior year in high school. I wasn't exactly sure what I wanted to do with my life at that point, but I knew I had a purpose. I no longer wanted to be high, hungover, or miss more opportunities.

I knew in my heart that my season of being a rebel was exactly that, a season, and deep in my heart I believed and envisioned a bright vision for the future. I decided to buckle down, get my act together, and graduate to move forward with the next stage of my life. Part of the drive to not only graduate but complete high school early was that I was finally ready to leave the adolescent rebellious years behind me and step into a new story—a story of achievement, accomplishment, and attainment.

During the transition of letting go of my breaking and delinquent behavior to growing up, maturing, getting my shit together, and applying for college, I was losing many friends or moving away from the peers I was close to. I was growing apart from this group of people because of their not-so-positive extracurricular activities, which I used to enjoy myself.

I started thinking about the long-term consequences of my actions and felt as if many of my peers were content with not moving forward in their lives. Additionally, I knew my interests were changing. I found a drive inside I had never known before, and I simply did not have free time to hang out or party because I was hustling to graduate a semester early.

Butterfly Effect

The way I've always understood the term butterfly effect is that one decision or one different turn could cause a completely different domino effect in your life. Have you ever asked yourself questions such as, "If I had not moved, how would my life have been different? "What about if I had never met my partner. What would be different? What if I had taken a different job, or what if I had studied something else?"

I strongly believe that everything happens for a reason and that every life event has set me up for the next; however, I often reflect on if I could go back, what would be different, and why? While sometimes we don't know it at the time, often we can look back and recognize that if an incident or choice didn't occur, another experience wouldn't have happened.

It's the epitome of the butterfly effect. In the fall of 2000, when I made the decision to graduate, I had zero idea of what would happen just a few months later; however, to this day, I know in my heart, gut, and entire body that choosing to graduate early was one of the best decisions I have ever made.

I am not sure if you have ever felt like you were being *led* (spiritually), but this is one of a handful of times I felt a pull so strong I knew it was not only the right decision but that something bigger and more powerful was behind it. I couldn't have planned to graduate early from the beginning, but looking back, I feel it was not by accident I was ignited to graduate early.

Traumatized Victim to Commander

Many of my friends were older and had already graduated or moved away, but my very best friend, Mary Rogers, was in my graduating class. Mary and I had been friends for years and did *everything* together. We shopped at the mall, went to parties, went to dances together, and told each other everything. The interesting thing about our friendship was that our personalities could not have been any more dichotomous.

I was known as the high school bully, the mean girl, and the one who intimidated everyone. Mary was known as the sweet girl, bubbly, kind, and *everyone* loved her. Many of our peers were nice or polite to me, maybe because they were afraid of me, while our entire class genuinely loved and adored Mary. She was the type of person who could make anyone smile, change the spirit of a room, and easily share her contagious laugh.

During the fall semester of our senior year, Mary and I started growing apart. I was taking extra classes and Mary was still partying, actually more than ever before. While I was trying to make up all of my high school credits in one semester, Mary was at raves, missing school, and talking about dropping out of school.

Our paths were headed in two dramatically different directions. Toward the end of the semester, shortly before winter break, I started reaching out to her more, trying to get some quality time, knowing that I was moving away to college after the holidays. I hoped for some time with my bestie before I left. Our friendship had changed, but in my heart, she was still my best friend. We made plans to go to coffee, but when I called to confirm the time and location that day, she blew me off. I was so frustrated and sad, and in a really bitchy and cold tone, I said,

"When you have time between doing drugs and selling drugs, call me."

Later that evening, my high school boyfriend and I drove about an hour away to housesit for some family friends of his. When we woke up in the morning, my pager was exploding. I remember having numerous messages with the code 911, and knew right away something was terribly wrong.

I called a close friend who had paged me. Her words will never leave my memory and they still chill my bones today. "Have you heard from Mary?" I told her no, and she shared with me that Mary had left the house where they were partying last night and never came back.

She told me they all had tried calling her, but got no response. She also informed me the news was covered with stories about a missing girl murdered the night before. Although the victim wasn't identified yet, the apartment complex on the news was not only a complex where another one of our friends lived, but it was also where Mary said she was going when she left the party.

I knew in every cell of my body, with every inch of my skin, the missing girl was my best friend, and I was frozen. Thousands of thoughts raced through my mind: anger, sadness, guilt, fear, a *lot* of fear, but the one thought that haunts me today, almost 20 years later, was, *Who is going to tell her mom? Someone has to tell Cindy, someone has to call her.* I took a few deep breaths and made the hardest phone call I have ever had to make. I called Mary's home and her mom answered. The first question I asked was, "Is Mary there?" I was hoping and praying that Mary was home and in such a deep sleep she had simply ignored all of her pages.

Her mom told me that she was not there and she never came home the night before. The second question I asked Mary's mom was, "Have you seen the news?" Cindy told me she hadn't seen the news. My lips quivered, my stomach flipped, my mouth was so dry I could barely speak, and with every ounce of strength I had, I said, "A young girl was murdered last night, and we think it may be Mary." I remember telling Cindy what I learned about Mary leaving and never coming back, how we knew the apartment complex that was on the news, and that she had been unresponsive for more than 12 hours.

To this day I have no idea what her mom felt during our call, but I experienced nausea, guilt, and fear like never before. What 17-year-old takes on the responsibility to make a phone call like that? I was so deeply devastated that a young girl, my *best friend*, had just lost her life, but I also sensed an overwhelming feeling of responsibility, literally convicting me that I could've done something.

Deep inside my gut, my heart, and my brain, I felt at fault, as if I didn't intervene enough or fight hard enough to help her. Even the day before, I could have said something, anything that would've possibly led to a different outcome than her death. While I recognize Mary's death was not my fault, the last words I said to her haunted me for months and years to come, and honestly, still bother me today.

The 'what if' story plays. What if I had just picked her up for coffee and didn't call to confirm? What if I had been a "snitch" and told her mom she was doing drugs? What if I had been *vulnerable* and instead of getting defensive I had actually said, "I miss you, and I am leaving soon, and I really want to spend time with you." It may not have changed the outcome of the events that evening, but that is a question I will never fully know the answer to.

Guilt is an unpredictable feeling. Many of us don't feel the guilt when we truly wrong others. In many other cases, we instead feel buried in guilt when we can't explain what happened: *What could I have done differently?* I don't know if I will always feel guilty in some way when I think of Mary, but what I do know is that there is still time for each of us to intervene, to simply *be* there for each other.

Is my success driven by guilt about Mary? No, but it's because of the memories of who she was to me and everything she taught me that I want to see others enjoy their closest friends and family members. I also learned early on that life can be very short and tomorrow is not promised. I vowed to myself to always be truthful with others, even when it hurts, and to *never* have bad goodbyes.

Grieving "Guest" to Overachiever

In my high school, the first semester of the school year finished after the holiday break, so students left for Christmas vacation, and came back after the New Year to finish finals. In my pursuit to graduate high school a semester early, and begin college right after the holiday break, I had to complete all of my high school finals before the holidays of my senior year. I was not only graduating early, but I was making up for so many missed classes and credits, and in less time than most, because I was planning on heading to college the next semester. The pursuit to graduate early was not only to get out of high school early but also to kick-start the next phase.

In my final few weeks of living in my hometown, and living at my parents' house before I went away to college, I never imagined coping with my best friend's murder as well. My last day of high school was Friday, December 15, 2000. Mary died Monday, January 8, 2001. Her funeral was the following Sunday, January 14, 2001, and I entered my first college lecture Sociology 101 on Monday, January 15, 2001. Needless to say, the grieving process was abrupt, the transition was massive, and the ramifications crippled me in the coming months.

I was accepted to Colorado State University as a part of their Guest Program, which is a delicate way of saying I was on academic probation. The difference is that academic probation only happens once you are a student, and you receive a warning, where the Guest Program is for new students who are accepted on a probationary status for their first year. I was so grateful to graduate high school early, and even have the opportunity to apply to a university, but my anything-but-stellar GPA and ACT and SAT scores traveled with me. It was a privilege to be considered; however, I knew it was conditional.

As a student in the Guest Program, I could attend classes but couldn't play sports or participate in extracurricular activities until I *earned* that privilege. I had to complete a semester and achieve a minimum of a 3.0 to receive full student body access. I knew I had something to *prove* as this former high school delinquent was now on her race to be a successful adult, and this gave me the motivation to show everyone I could do it.

Additionally, my dad and stepmom were investing in me, and since they weren't the most supportive of me graduating high school early, I definitely did not want to disappoint them. I was fixated on becoming a successful college freshman and exemplifying that I deserved to be there, but at the time, I was not aware of the emotion I would bury, grieving the loss of Mary, in trying to be a normal college student, as well as the fear, anxiety, and Post-Traumatic Stress Disorder (PTSD) waiting to explode in my life.

FINDING MY STRENGTH

I think we innately expect good things to happen to good people and assume bad things happen to bad people. At least that's the way the movies make it, right? Whether you know someone who had cancer, was in a horrible car accident, or went through a natural disaster, it is natural to wonder why that happened to them.

One of the hardest things for me about Mary's murder was that I knew her perpetrator, and there was nothing alarming about him. Sean was not necessarily making the best choices. He was a drug addict and was selling and doing drugs, but he wasn't someone I would have described as violent or scary. When he killed Mary, Two fears exploded in my mind and took years to heal, forgive, and grieve through.

The first was: *It could have been me.* I think about all the poor choices our group of friends was making then. It could've happened to any one of us. Mary wasn't doing anything differently and assuredly wasn't at all deserving. In actuality, it was quite the opposite, as she was the sweetest gal on earth, gentle, joyful, happy, and uplifting.

The second fear was: *How do I trust people again?* If we missed red flags about Sean, or even worse, if he didn't have any, how in the world would I ever trust again? How could you tell good people from bad people? I didn't want to go through life living in fear, however, after she died I found myself looking for problems with people, focusing on imperfections or idiosyncrasies, or innately shielding myself against them, instead of focusing on their qualities, gifts, and trusting that most people have good intentions.

****

Have you ever experienced a panic attack? Have you ever seen someone have a panic attack? Have you ever felt anxiety so powerful that even though every ounce of your mind and body knows the fear or phobia is irrational, the emotion still dictates your life?

That was my first year of college.

I look back and think how often I loosely used the word *panic...* before I ever truly experienced it. I remember driving one day to class and having an uncontrollable amount of racing thoughts. Every single day, hour, and moment our brains are processing so much information, but this was a completely different feeling. It was unique because every thought coming through my mind was negative, "what if this happened" type of thinking. In the one- to two-mile drive to campus, I felt as if there were *thousands* of thoughts. *"What happens if you get sick in the car?" "What happens if you get sick in class?" "What will people think of you?" "Who will clean it up?" "Who will take you home?"*

In addition to the thoughts, I remember my stomach in knots, my palms sweaty, losing peripheral vision, and feeling as if I only had tunnel vision. The worst part was a tightness around my upper chest and neck that literally left me out of breath. It's not the same feeling as being choked, but the pressure and tightness around my throat were debilitating. Just before I got to school, the fear of something happening to me and the fear of no one being there to take care of me was enough for me to turn the car around, go home, and crawl into bed. I was so motivated to get to college and so excited to finally be *choosing* to go to class, but I was hindered by this disorder.

After a few minutes, maybe an hour after this occurred, I started feeling better. That's when the cycle of beating myself up began. *What the f**k is wrong with you, Lauren? Why don't you go to class like everyone else? You aren't ready for college, Lauren, you're so paranoid you can't even get to class. You've been a liar and a delinquent your whole life, no one is going to believe you! They're just going to say they told you that you aren't ready.*

I was proving everyone else right... I couldn't do it... *I wasn't good enough.*

Often when someone suffers from extreme anxiety, phobias develop as a way to control the nervous energy and feel like you are finding control over something you actually cannot control. For me specifically, I developed a fear of throwing up that literally would immobilize me in certain situations. I felt paralyzed in life due to this overbearing fear.

Anxiety is often triggered by situations in which a person feels out of control. Furthermore, phobias are often irrational, but to the person experiencing the phobia, the fear feels very real. Each individual's behavior can vary based on the severity of the phobia, but it's important to recognize how powerful the mind is, so no matter how irrational a fear or phobia may be, to the person experiencing the fear it can seem incredibly real, terrifying, and in some cases, truly interferes with one's life.

A childhood experience came back to haunt me during my freshman year in college when I was struggling with PTSD, anxiety, and agoraphobia, which is the fear of leaving your home. One weekend when we were kids, Rachael and I were at our dad's house. We ate at a restaurant before he took us home to mom's house that night. A few hours later both Rachael and I were tremendously sick. We were very young, early elementary school age, and definitely struggling to make it to the bucket, let alone the bathroom.

I remember two things. The first was that I couldn't help vomiting and I had zero control over what my body was experiencing. What was happening to my body was something I had never felt before and there was no such thing as being able to hold it. The second was the frustration of my mom. She was the best when we were sick (colds, strep, ear infections, chicken pox), but she didn't deal with stomach illness well.

While she never meant to come off this way, I remember feeling so shameful. This was also in the middle of divorce hell so I'm sure the emotional stress was high. That being said, still today, I hear the sarcastic remarks that were made, the tone of what was said for something that wasn't our *fault*. Comments were made such as, "their dad had fun with the girls all weekend and brought them back to us like this!"

I remember feeling so embarrassed and so dependent. This was the last time I've ever experienced the stomach flu or vomited under any circumstances, all through middle school, high school, and actually still today in my mid-30s, but ultimately, it was the trigger behind my phobia. This obsession over *What if I get sick?* was exactly the fear I couldn't control, so I found myself in obsessive controlling patterns, trying to control what I couldn't control as a release of the anxiety I was experiencing.

A psychologist that I worked with at the time explained my phobia was less about the vomiting experience and more about me being out of control, and needing the help of others. Additionally, because it had been so long since I had been sick, it was a fear of not knowing what to expect. This is not the sexiest topic to discuss, but it's important to know I wasn't scared of choking as much as I was scared of not being able to take care of myself or get through it alone.

I had become accustomed to doing everything on my own, but *what if* I needed help? Who would be there? The deeper fear was my lack of trust in people and the doubt that someone could love me enough to take care of me, clean up my mess, and not judge me if I needed help. In many situations to come, including car rides, flights, large classroom lectures, going to work, or even the grocery store, this fear would arise. Panic attacks were a regular part of my schedule during this time in my life and an upset stomach, someone else's upset stomach, new restaurants, and confined spaces were often the triggers.

The phobias were real and dictating my life; however, the lack of confidence and worthiness lingered long after the panic attacks stopped. Those are the drivers that propelled me to keep reaching for help and motivated me to get better. I *knew* this wasn't the strong, independent gal who just graduated early from high school. This was the suffocating side effect of childhood trauma and multiple traumatic experiences that all culminated with Mary's murder.

Anxiety and Relationships

While trying to combat these major mental traumas, and protect my ego from admitting to my parents I was struggling, I developed a very codependent relationship with my high school sweetheart and college boyfriend, Duncan. Anxiety and PTSD are weird; somewhere in my fears and mistrust of humans, I became obsessively trusting of him. Not only did I view him as a *safe* person, but I relied on him for everything. Our friends called us mashup nicknames of our first names (Laur-Dunc or Du-Lauren) because we were inseparable.

While many thought it was because we were young and in love, it was really because he provided comfort and security. I didn't feel like I could do things without him. From relatively small tasks such as going to class or the grocery store to more intermediate levels of challenge, such as driving an hour-and-a-half home to visit our families, I began to tell myself a story, that if Duncan was there, everything would be OK. I had gone through life for so long taking care of Lauren, not fully trusting anyone, solely relying on myself sometimes, and suddenly, I felt like I couldn't do anything unless he was there.

So often we've heard the saying, "Don't put all your eggs in one basket." As an 18-year-old girl, that is exactly what I did. I relied on him so much that not only did my codependency perpetuate my distrust in other people, but it also pushed him away. How could a young man possibly carry so much pressure and responsibility? Duncan had a part-time job at a local restaurant, like most normal college kids. He would go to work for a few hours, which often felt like days for me. While he was serving and making extra cash, I was doing my best to focus on my academics.

I also was not the typical college kid when it came to partying. While many of my peers were experimenting with drugs for the first time or enjoying the college specials at the local bars, I was busy burying myself in studying. Since I made the decision to get sober at the end of high school, I was still abstaining from everything. I never touched drugs again, but I also stayed away from alcohol, even once I was of legal age. It wasn't that I was simply too anxious and afraid of being out of control if I drank, but I was too focused and committed to my goals.

I was so obsessed with convincing everyone (including myself) that I wasn't going to flunk out that I literally didn't have time to party. This part of the story is important to know because I wasn't the fun girl that Duncan had met in high school. I was a college freshman trapped in anxiety and obsessive-compulsive controlling patterns.

I was so scared on many nights. Anxiety would take over, and I would curl up and just cry, waiting for him to come home so that I knew *everything was going to be OK.* On the flip side, Duncan was experiencing freedom, fun, and living life as a normal college kid should. While he was finding a social life, the dichotomy was that, while he was out having fun, I was restlessly waiting for him to come home, like an anxious puppy.

He ended up falling in love with a hostess from the restaurant. When I found out, I was crushed. Not only did I lose the *one* person I completely relied on, but this heartbreak also fueled my story of once again not being able to trust people, and also fueled my story of not being good enough. Time and time again, I've seen good people get hurt, and I too have been hurt, especially by people who supposedly loved me, and I found myself in very uncomfortable, but familiar territory... *on the curb.*

Those closest to me describe me as a positive person, as someone who always finds the bright side, and no matter how difficult the challenge, obstacle, or tragedy, I always find a way to triumph. What once was one of the biggest heartaches I ever experienced, something that evoked such bitterness in my heart, has now become one of the best blessings in disguise. As

Garth Brooks says, "Some of God's greatest gifts are unanswered prayers." At one point I had our entire future mapped out, and that door slammed shut so strongly, I was forced to see what new doors opened.

I had prayed and prayed that my now-former boyfriend and I would end up happily ever after, mostly because I felt like I *needed* him, and that unanswered prayer was critical in the direction change my life was headed. The distrust of cheating men didn't heal immediately; it actually haunted me for many years to come; however, losing him helped me regain my independence, forced me to decide who I was and who I wanted to be, and ultimately brought me back to life, knowing I had no one to lean on like that anymore. I was committed to getting healthy, and mentally well. I had the motto, *If life is going to be, it is going to be up to me!* I wasn't going to rely on anyone to do things for me and was willing to do whatever it took to heal.

Letting Go—Choosing Joy

I decided I wanted to travel abroad after college graduation. I wasn't off getting married or starting a family and I knew that this was the time in my life to make it happen. Breaking up with my high school boyfriend was an unanswered prayer, part of which was finding this drive to travel, embrace the zest of life, and find me again.

After graduating I would have eight or nine months off from school before starting my master's degree. I knew in my heart that if I didn't go then, I might not ever go. When would I not have classes, a job, a family, or other responsibilities so I could freely take off? I committed to doing it. Throughout my senior year, I worked as a server and also did some private tutoring and nannying to save money for my upcoming trip.

I knew I was going alone, and after so recently overcoming my agoraphobia, I wanted the comfort of going to an English-speaking country. All three of my older sisters traveled, and I wanted to go somewhere new, somewhere no one in the family had been, so I chose New Zealand and Australia.

For months I researched cities, hostels, and possible excursions, and knew that if I could just get there, actually get on the plane, I would be just fine. I found my outgoing personality again after coming a long way with my PTSD, anxiety, and fears of trusting people; however, I was often still paralyzed with my fear of throwing up. Every time I got excited about the trip, I got equally nervous about the 18-hour flight, and specifically, my irrational phobia of *What happens if I get sick on the plane?*

For my college graduation present, my dad and stepmom gifted me upgraded seats. Instead of flying coach, I was flying first-class from Denver to San Francisco, and business class from San Francisco to Sydney and then to Auckland. I was blown away and humbled by their generosity, grateful knowing I would be more comfortable. I kept telling myself, *Everything is going to be OK... this is a trip of a lifetime.*

My dad and stepmom took me to the airport and walked me to security as far as they could go. I remember them crying and I surely was crying. I was trying to be tough, a brave young woman, a girl who had just finished two bachelor's degrees with a minor in four years, and regained her confidence and independence. I was the girl everyone said couldn't do it, and now, I was doing it. I was too scared to look back and just kept walking through the security line like the little engine that could, *I think I can... I think I can... I think I can,* as I was embarking on a trip that would change my life.

Let me remind you that this was in 2004 before everyone had cell phones glued to their hands, and surely before international calling plans were as common as they are today. I had a backpack holding everything I would need for the next few months, a passport carrier around my neck with traveler's checks, cash, my passport, and my calling cards. I got to the gate, but was too shy to go into the United Club because I thought, *How many young travelers are flying first class?* Instead, I patiently waited to board the flight.

I was flying to San Francisco from Denver, about a two-hour flight, and I knew my sister and brother-in-law were waiting for me there. Rachael was currently living in the Bay area and was coming to see me during my layover. I sat at the gate shaking, palms sweating, mouth dry, and crocodile tears pooling in my eyes. I thought about where I was as a 17-year-old girl, the delinquent who almost didn't graduate. I thought about how far I had come by 21, and just said, Pull *up your big-girl pants, get on that plane, and let's do this!*

Remember, just months before, I was petrified to drive, let alone fly. Keep in mind that not only had it been a while since I had flown, but I had *never* flown alone. I remember getting on the plane, turning down *all* of the first class food and alcohol options, listening to my iPod, and beginning to journal. While I was so scared and so nervous, I also knew I was leaving a part of my past behind me, and that I would never be the same once I returned.

I landed in San Francisco and couldn't wait to see Rachael and her boyfriend Jay, (now her husband). We hung out in the main concourse for a few hours. I remember Rach trying to calm me down, and in her naturally logical way printed off a list of all of the ways more common to die than in a plane crash. While my fear wasn't actually flying, I appreciated her effort.

My brother-in-law, who's always been like a real big brother to me, had a surprise for me. About a year before, I flew to Florida with my best friend for spring break. At the time, I had this little white teddy bear I took with me everywhere. OK, not everywhere, but more places than a college girl should take a stuffed animal. I know it sounds childish, but it was something that calmed me, something I could fidget with, and most of all, offered peace of mind. Our flight was full of turbulence, so many passengers were sick around us, and I actually ripped one of the legs off the teddy because I was so scared.

So, Jay pulls his gift for me out of a bag—a bright blue stuffed octopus. With a very loving and teasing expression, he said, "Now you have eight legs to rip off." While most college graduates would be horrified to carry a stuffed octopus into business class of a 777, I couldn't have been more grateful.

The time came to say goodbye to Rachael and Jay, and once again, I headed to the gate. It was around 6:30 p.m. I have never before felt the way I did then. My legs were like lead, they were so heavy. My heart raced as if I had just sprinted up a mountain. My hands were so clammy I couldn't even hold my boarding pass.

I remember barely being able to swallow, my stomach turning and turning, and felt frozen as if I couldn't move. While I wanted to imagine meeting amazing people from all over the world, picturing the glaciers I was going to climb, and the reefs I was going to dive, all I could think about was, *What happens if I get sick on this plane? Who will take care of me? What if I can't make it to the bathroom?*

I faintly remember someone saying my name. Then the airline attendant actually walked over to me. She said, "Are you, Miss Danielle?" I could barely get the words out, so I nodded my head yes. She told me they were doing final boarding and they had called my name three times. She said, "We're going to need you to come on board." While I felt as if there were a thousand pounds of bricks on my chest, and every bit of me wanted to go home and sheepishly admit that I *couldn't do it,* I knew in my core this was going to be a pivotal time in my life. I told myself the same mantra I had been saying for months. *All you have to do is get there... What's the worst that could happen? Stop worrying... Start doing... You can do this!*

I grabbed my backpack and new octopus and boarded the plane. As I walked up the stairs to the upper deck and took my seat, I was overwhelmed with gratitude. I started to calm down, started to experience the moment, and decided that if I kept living in fear, I'd always be missing out. If I started to let go and just *be;* the whole world was in my hands.

Many people have heard the saying the FEAR is simply False Evidence Appearing Real, which leaves you with two choices:

1. Forget Everything And Run or
2. Face Everything And Rise.

Before we took off I committed to YOLO—you only live once! I knew I was off on an adventure that only a small percentage of people get to experience. No way was I was letting a phobia or past story of who I was dictate my trip. Almost with the snap of a finger, I started breaking free. I started to trust. I started to let go. Most importantly, I started opening up the first layer of my incredibly hard, sturdy, and unbreakable shell.

Kia Ora—To Live

I knew I had passion. I knew I was on a mission to find my purpose, and I knew I was meant for more. I also had an innate understanding that it was going to take work; however, I became relentless in my pursuit to be successful, eliminate my fears, and start living life to the fullest.

Within this transformation I started saying "Yes!" to many of the things I had been saying "No" to throughout my undergraduate years. While I was traveling abroad, any time I wanted to do something but got nervous or anxious, I had a mantra that I would tell myself, which ultimately got me to pull up my big girl panties and "Just do it!" I would say, *You only live once. You are safe. Everything you've ever needed or wanted is already inside of you, so let's live life to the fullest and do this!*

Have you ever created a mantra for your life? Tony Robbins, the motivational speaker and coach, speaks on getting into the right state of mind. Sometimes even having a power move to elevate your activity and emotional response can activate the right state of mind. It's fun to see how I taught myself this as a young adult, perfected it on my personal growth journey, and found a deep passion today showing others how to do this. Visualizing what you want is one of the first steps to overcoming any fear or limitation holding you back.

I think about the college girl who struggled to go to the grocery store alone because she was so scared. Now here I was, on the other side of the world, a completely different hemisphere, meeting people from all over the world, doing incredibly brave and adventurous activities, sleeping in hostels, and feeling completely *free* for the first time ever. When I reminisce about this trip, I remember skydiving over Lake

Taupo, climbing a massive glacier in a blizzard, getting my scuba diving certification in the middle of the ocean (with people I had just met that day in a dive shop), sleeping in random hostels every night, and riding a bus all around two countries by myself, seeing as much as I could.

While these experiences were incredible, memorable, once-in-a-lifetime moments, the part of the trip that leaves the most lasting impression was the sense of freedom. It's the belief that "I can _____!" Kia Ora ... To Live! Even if it was just for a few months, I felt confident, loved, fearless, proud, and ignited. I knew there was good in people and so much more to life than I previously thought.

I also started to realize my unique gifts. While I was meeting people from all around the world, on buses, at excursions, or in hostels, I could tell they were taking as much interest in getting to know me as I was in getting to know them. I remember for the first time seeing people for who they are and being seen for who I am, as opposed to seeing people with past stories, labels, or status. Maybe it was the state of mind or the magical location, but I will never forget that it felt like a no judgment zone. The months I spent there increased my confidence, eliminated past stories, and opened my heart to possibility, to opportunity, and to joy, a feeling I hadn't experienced in years.

When I think about New Zealand, what I remember most is finding my inner child again. After Mary's murder, I became so hypervigilant and anxious, I wasn't just living in constant worry and fear, but I also wasn't having fun. I remember feeling safe in New Zealand and also playful, joyful, and trusting. Sometimes when I think about why I felt safe it's challenging to say because it seems so "woo woo," but the vibe and energy of the culture felt different to me.

Almost immediately upon arriving in New Zealand, I could sense that the priority was on people, not possessions or status. It was evident in conversations that the value of relationships and experiences far outweighed owning things or anything materialistic. It felt like I was living in another time period, but the kinships and obvious sense that people wanted to support others provided a security blanket for me as I was embarking alone on foreign travel.

As a kid (OK, even as an adult) I was so worried about what others would think that I often didn't try new things. As a teenager I was so preoccupied with being a bully or making poor decisions that I missed out on many kid moments, just playing or simply being. In college I was an overachieving stress ball, trying to prove something to everyone, including myself, that I didn't experience some of the silliness or fun times as I was racing to accomplish something bigger and better. I think of intramural activities, theme parties, or mud runs I was too busy or, honestly, too uncomfortable to do, and sadly missed out on great times. Remember how liberating it was for me to skip?

New Zealand offered a sense of freedom, a you-only-live-once attitude, and the ability to just *be*. Writing about the stories now still brings a smile to my face and calmness to my heart, knowing that when I was down under, I *lived*, I said yes to everything I wanted to do, and I didn't let fear, my comfort zone, or the opinions of others interfere with my dreams, goals, aspirations, or experiences. That's where I found my strength.

Where in your life are you holding back? What moments are you saying no to that you wish you were saying yes to? A cliché question we've all heard, "If today was your last day, how would you spend it?" While I am not suggesting we play to that extreme, I am encouraging you to be present more, to take chances, to take risks, and to embark on experiences that are not always readily available. Many elderly people have reported that if they could do things over, they would have said yes to more experiences. Be brave! Be open! Take the leap!

FROM CRIMINAL JUSTICE TO COMPETITIVE CATALYST

Criminal Justice

As an undergraduate student, I studied psychology, sociology, and criminal justice. I kept thinking that if someone had intervened in Mary's life or her killer's life, maybe she would still be here today. I also frequently reflected on teachers, family members, and counselors who subtly redirected me back to the right path, and had an overwhelming feeling to wanting to give back, to help others get off the beaten path. Sometimes when young adults go to college, they have no clue what they want to do, but I had a clear vision. I was going to be a correctional officer like Ms. Johnson, from the movie *Dangerous Minds*. In the movie, actress Michelle Pfeiffer plays a former U.S. Marine, who helps her students gain confidence, believe in themselves, and find their greatest potential. I was on a mission to stop teen crime, my way of making the world a better place.

While I loved my undergraduate studies and my internship at the Division of Youth Corrections, things suddenly changed as soon as I got to graduate school. I had graduated from college and knew that if I wanted to have any type of authority in the field, or advance above the base pay level, graduate school was a must. I went on to pursue a master's degree in criminal justice.

In the very first class, the professor explained that there were three paths we would most likely choose upon graduation: law enforcement, judicial, or corrections. While my heart had always been in corrections, I suddenly was losing my passion for Ms. Johnson. Part of the change was my own healing journey and my growth since my rebel days. I was in my 20s now, and not only had I been to therapy, and I had grieved the loss of my friend, (not that it ever goes away, but I was no longer struggling with PTSD). I had also just come back from a life-changing trip in New Zealand that opened my heart and mind to so many different ways of life, types of people, and avenues I had not previously considered.

At the same time, I was falling out of love with a career in Criminology. I was being introduced to the health and wellness industry, and I suddenly had a drastic change of heart about the profession I wanted to take. I went on to complete my degree, (c'mon, Lauren Danielle is not a quitter!). However, I never went into criminal justice as a career.

I was falling in love with fitness, nutrition, and a completely different way of impacting lives. My health and wellness career began in group fitness and personal training, but I quickly learned I couldn't teach group fitness classes full time. While I would love to be able to work out all day, every day, that is not sustainable, so I went on to pursue a second master's degree in clinical nutrition.

Don't be surprised that *once again* Lauren was changing her path, or going against the norm. I mean seriously, who finishes a master's, and dives right into another one? But I *knew* this was the right decision. My drive to help others and impact lives was congruent; however, I was realizing I wanted to be more proactive, and less reactive. The corrections field is dealing with the aftermath of poor decisions. Not to say that preventative programs don't exist, but the career I had chosen was on the other side. Similarly, when I think of the healthcare system, too often we are actually managing sick care as opposed to actually educating and promoting health.

My drive to pursue a career in nutrition was multifaceted. I could create an income that didn't require the physical demands on my body that fitness classes did. I could make a difference in people's lives to help them choose to live a healthy life without waiting for a health scare, so often, I find people (including myself), reacting to situations, as opposed to preparing and planning ahead to avoid certain scenarios.

I had no clue that my criminal justice path would lead me here, but back to the butterfly effect, had I not moved to Arizona, I may have never joined the gym I did, where I met my first group fitness boss, who mentored me and taught me how to lead group fitness classes. It never ceases to amaze me how certain choices, decisions, and paths, are always leading us to exactly where we are meant to be.

Competitive Catalyst

I was very active in sports and competitions growing up. My sister and I played hopscotch, tetherball, and rode our bikes everywhere. As a kid I danced, jumped rope, and played soccer. In middle school I ran track, where I was actually quite good, attempted to play volleyball, and continued to play competitive soccer; however, by the time I got to high school, weed, cigarettes, alcohol, and playing video games with my friends unfortunately became my extracurricular activities. With the exception of an occasional hike, or walk around the mall, I was lazy, sedentary, and lost my drive for most physical activity. It took years to reignite this flame.

My first semester at Colorado State University was transformational. Not only was I passionately pursuing my undergraduate education, but I also no longer wanted to be the 'bad kid.' I was exhausted from going against the grain and wanted to be a part of the student body. Not only did I feel like I had something to *prove*, and I actually became very driven and competitive with my academics, but I also wanted to make some health changes.

I was a part of an honor society and *hated* that I was the only smoker in the group. What was once *cool* to be a part of, the crowd that smoked, was now embarrassing to me. I had many classes on the third and fourth floors of the Clark building on campus, and I can recall being winded and out of breath every day walking up those stairs. I also knew that as a 17-year-old college freshman, the Colorado altitude was *not* the problem.

A good friend knew I wanted to make some changes, and she invited me to join her at the recreation center. I wasn't familiar with most of the gym equipment and didn't know where to start. I started working out with her simply to have a starting point and some accountability, but it wasn't fun. The types of exercise we were doing, the circuit equipment, and the monotonous elliptical machine were beyond boring. I was incredibly deconditioned that everything we did was so hard!

I remember staring at the timer on the elliptical and thinking, *This is the longest 30 minutes of my life.* I knew if I wanted to get healthy, exercise wasn't going to be enough, and I also had to quit smoking. In May of 2001, I made the decision to quit smoking and have never touched a cigarette since.

While that was extraordinary, the other news was that I gained over 40 pounds in record time. I replaced my morning cigarette with sweets, drive-time cigarettes with candy, and after-dinner cigarettes with TCBY white chocolate mousse and Ben and Jerry's cookie and cream ice cream. At nearly 200 pounds, even though I was smoke-free, I was borderline obese. I needed to make serious changes.

I hired a personal trainer for the first time ever and started taking Les Mills group fitness classes. This was the beginning of me truly falling in love with the health and wellness industry. I enjoyed being pushed and challenged by instructors. I was so happy when I started seeing results and my transformation. I truly looked forward to my BODYPUMP™, RPM™, BODYCOMBAT, and BODYATTACK™ classes.

I found myself planning the group fitness classes into my calendar and also building a new community of supportive, positive, and encouraging friends. These classes started my days with positivity, drive, and adrenaline, or ended my days as a stress reliever and a way to manage daily overwhelm. It was also fun to see familiar faces and embrace this new community, something I never had before. I also was not good at very many things growing up. I got kicked out of band camp (for breaking the rules), cut from the A soccer team, and flunked more classes than I passed, but suddenly, fitness was my jam!

Not only was fitness something I truly enjoy and I'm passionate about, but I was really good at being fit. I found myself in the front row, gaining confidence, and pushing myself harder than I ever had. I found coordination, rhythm, strength, and endurance and was feeling accomplished. My dad was an all-star athlete, and I started thinking, *Do I have his genes? Could I actually do something in the realm of fitness?* Thank goodness I said yes, because not only did fitness create another turning point in my life, but I also had some of the best fitness mentors a newbie could ever ask for, which launched a now 18-year career.

Addicted to Transformation

Everything in your life has gotten you to where you are right now. I adore so many parts of the fitness industry—the transformations, the competitiveness, the music, the energy, but the area of fitness I fell head over heels in love with was watching people blossom from the inside out. So often when people lose weight, it's as if a new person emerges, the one who was buried under extra pounds.

I didn't know at the time how addicted I would become to seeing other's transformations and wanting to be a catalyst of change for them. I recognized myself as a leader and started to see myself as a person who could inspire, motivate, and impact others. When I think of what I get to do today, I realize everything perfectly set me up for this moment since my background in health and wellness is advantageous for my success.

Additionally, it was a pivotal time in my life when I started believing in myself. I had a repeating story in my head for years that I wasn't good enough or I was the bad kid, so who was going to listen to me? When I recognized that people were actually trusting me, respecting me, and I was the one paving the way, it began to shift how I saw myself. This ultimately started to change how I see my potential, as well as what distinguishes me from others in the industry.

If you've ever been on a weight-loss journey or any type of physical transformation, then you know how much emotion is stirred up and released in the process. We all have relationships with food. It's how we are taught to celebrate, cope, and even make it through tough days. In many ways, food is an outlet when it comes to grief and stress. While I signed up to be a personal trainer and nutritionist and thought I would just use science to make plans, I had no idea how much psychology would come into play.

The emotional component of this profession is the part I fell in love with the most. While seeing bodies transform excited me, watching breakthroughs of past stories or seeing clients smash self-limiting beliefs ignited me. This was the start to me of finding my calling to scale this passion and gift at a much larger level. I knew training clients one-on-one was limiting my reach, and I was so obsessed with catapulting this time of change, I knew there would be another way for me to do what I love: guiding people to their ideal life but on a much larger scale.

Significance: Natural Leader

From the time I committed to graduating high school early until my late 20s, even into my early 30s, I never took my foot off the gas. I was go - go - go - go and go some more. I grew accustomed to running around, racing from job to job, completing project after project, acquiring degree after degree, and getting consumed by drama upon drama.

As exhausting as this sounds, it was a way of life for me. With two master's degrees, two bachelor's degrees, and nearly

$100,000 in debt, I was working my tail off, burnt out, frustrated, and had nothing to show for it. Looking back, I remember this innate drive to be more and do more, even when I wasn't trying to prove something. When I think about my personality in college and graduate school, I was incredibly bubbly and joyful and loving life, but upon graduating, I felt more overwhelmed, overworked, and exhausted than anything else.

I was the fitness instructor who showed up, turned the intensity to 11 on a scale of 1-10, and buried my own stress to ignite an entire classroom. I did this over 17 hours per week after working 40 hours in a doctor's office, 30 hours in my office, 20 hours at the restaurant, and so forth. In the midst of all of that, I was such a social butterfly, driving from job to job on the phone, listening to people's drama, trying to support and encourage everyone else, and needless to say, the Energizer Bunny™ was no longer energized.

I am sure you have heard of adrenal fatigue. Maybe you've experienced it yourself or know someone who has. Have you found yourself snapping for unexplained reasons, less patient or more tired than you used to be? I remember when these health terms were foreign to anyone not in the medical or holistic community and now they are mainstream to nearly everyone: adrenal stress, adrenal burnout, and emotional exhaustion are three of the many ways to describe this breakdown in the body. In caveman times, our adrenals were glands that helped us survive, literally our fight or flight organs. Today, they are in overdrive. Our adrenal responses used to happen in short bursts, rallying to help us survive, but today, they seem to never shut off.

Think about a time you were startled. Maybe you were nearly rear-ended or someone happened to scare you, and you felt that instant surge of adrenaline. That's your adrenals at work. Consider a time when you were so tired, but your mind just kept racing once you hit the pillow. At 11 o'clock at night you had more energy to complete everything you didn't have the energy to do all day.

These are just two of the many ways to prove our adrenals are working overtime, but ways our adrenals are activated when they shouldn't be. What was originally designed to keep us alive is now a detriment to so many people's health. Even though our minds can distinguish an early morning cardio workout from running from a bear in the woods, our bodies cannot. Similarly, our mind knows work deadlines won't kill us the same way falling off a cliff will, but the constant worry and stress break down our bodies.

Relationship stress, financial stress, overtraining our physical bodies, work stress, lack of sleep, and overuse of caffeine are a few ways we are taxing our adrenals every single day. Think about the number of people who experience ulcers or suffer heart attacks because of stress. There is no physical diagnosis, but we know it happens. Our day-to-day stress about money, kids, work, sleep, and fulfillment is often as crucial to our more visible health when it comes to protecting against major forms of illness or disease.

According to adrenalfatiguesolution.com, adrenal fatigue is "a stress-related condition that results in symptoms like exhaustion, weakened immunity, sleep disturbances, and food cravings. The adrenal glands... become depleted and dysregulated after a long period of emotional stress or chronic illness."[2] On the Mayo Clinic website, adrenal fatigue is described as "a term applied to a collection of nonspecific symptoms, such as body aches, fatigue, nervousness, sleep disturbances, and digestive problems."[3] As you can see, it's not an aggressive diagnosis necessarily, but rather a condition that our lifestyle causes, with symptoms that show up in all areas of life. What triggers our adrenals is crucial to understand if you want to live a long and healthy life.

In my early to mid-20s I knew I was experiencing adrenal fatigue. Not only was I gaining weight (again), feeling run down, frequently getting sick, struggling with sleep, and just edgy, but the two most popular words out of my mouth, when someone asked how I was doing, were tired or exhausted. It's no surprise why I was, but who wants to go through life simply so they can tell people how drained they are? I always knew I was made for something powerful. Innately I know that I am driven, I believe I can be a voice for others, and ultimately I'm drawn to make an impact. In the midst of job overwhelm, combined with a lack of fulfillment, passion, or purpose, I crossed paths with network marketing.

Network Marketing? Me?

Let me backtrack for a moment. Before joining my network marketing company, the only thing I knew about the industry was that I didn't like it. My naive assumptions, coupled with the rumors or stigmas I heard, pretty much negated this opportunity

---

[2] Adrenalfatiguesolution.com

[3] mayoclinic.com

for me. For years, I was introduced to a "life-changing opportunity," but all I saw were fake people chasing a dream with a lot of hype, and no one really succeeding.

I was often promised an incredible income, but what people didn't realize is that I wasn't chasing a paycheck. I was chasing a purpose, a vehicle to not only set myself free of financial stress but also a vehicle that could leverage my passion and reach way more people than I was currently seeing in my office with a rotating door of hourly clients, exchanging time for money.

Besides just the network marketing business presentations, I was invited to so many parties where I was being convinced to buy something I didn't even need—an extra bag, more mascara, new knives, kitchen gadgets, candles, travel memberships... *So Many. Parties.* I was always supportive of my friends and family, but I never left a party saying, *I can't wait for all of my friends and family to come over so I can sell them jewelry, or makeup.* The passion simply was not there for me.

In September 2013, shortly after my 30th birthday, my vanilla-flavored, mediocre, tiresome, burned-out life took a major turn (not for the better) in a very quick time. On a Friday afternoon, I paid off my quarterly taxes, which virtually wiped out my checking and savings accounts. When you are living paycheck to paycheck, it doesn't take much to run the well dry. Later that evening, I also found out that my dad had been diagnosed with Parkinson's disease.

I share this because even though Dad would've helped in a second, it was the first time in my life that I felt I had to figure it out on my own. I am the youngest of four girls, the only one not married, and if it was going to be, it was going to be up to me... Shit, I was 30!

The third thing that happened was my boyfriend, at that time of many years, broke up with me on the spot. I had moved in with him that summer, gotten rid of most of my belongings, and then he decided to call it quits within just a few months of moving in together, so, after paying my first and last month's rent, deposits, and so forth, I found myself with $17 to my name, in a brand-new apartment, with virtually nothing but clothes. Once again, I found myself in a very familiar and unsettling situation... *on the curb.* Instead of sitting on a cul-de-sac curb this time, I was on an unfurnished apartment floor, scared, lonely, and sad. *What is wrong with me? I asked. How could I be working so hard, be giving so much, and still be struggling like this?*

The broke and broken little girl in that apartment knew that if something was going to change, something had to change.

No way could I continue living the way I was if I wanted to live a different way. It was moments later when my real-life guardian angel called me. I will never forget the words that came out of her mouth, "Hi, it's Jani. I heard what happened to you and I can help you." What?!

I was guarded and defensive, surely not open or willing to be 'pitched', yet I innately trusted her, knew I had to do something different, and felt her passion and compassion, and I wanted what she had!

Jani asked me questions, opened my heart, and the timing was uncanny. Jani asked me about my life and helped me paint a vision for my future by getting me to think outside the box. She asked me what life would be like if I was not exchanging time for money or how it would feel to have a team of people who were like-minded, motivated, and working together for a greater purpose.

The most pivotal question she asked was, "What do you need most right now?" I needed so many things, but I told her, "A bed." I was on the apartment floor, shameful, and wanted to get back up on my feet. In addition to getting excited about a new way of life or having opportunities I had only dreamt about, but never believed would happen, I was ready. I was so frustrated with the life I was living, so desperate for a change that I would've said yes to almost anything.

The beauty and miracle of it all was that I was saying yes to a health and wellness company that was congruent with my nutritional standards. Their company core values at the time were better than my own personal values. I knew I was going to become the healthiest version of myself, impact thousands of lives, and in the process, design my life the way I had always imagined.

So many beautiful experiences have come from my network marketing career, including the freedom of no longer exchanging time for money and the ability to impact far more lives than I could in my little office by myself. The greatest impacts it has had on my life, outside of financial gains, are the journey of personal development, the relationships I've formed, the places I've traveled, and the freedom I've found.

Sometimes I reflect back on my life and ask questions such as: *What if I hadn't graduated high school early? What if I never started taking group fitness classes? What if my high school boyfriend and I didn't break up?* I have the racing butterfly effect story in my mind sometimes about how different my life would be if I made a different decision at a different time and always come up with the same answers. *Everything happens for a reason and everything leads you to exactly where you are supposed to be right now.*

Saying "Yes!" to network marketing became a vehicle where I would heal my not good enough story. This lifestyle is what brought me back to life from adrenal burnout, ignited my passion for helping others, aided in finding my purpose, and ultimately, turned on my Dreamer Light!

Success

When I look back, it's amazing how many things fell into place that perfectly set me up for where I am today. In hindsight, I couldn't have planned this journey on purpose, even if I tried. While I do not believe you need a background in health and wellness to be successful in a health and wellness network marketing company, I was so grateful to have a following in the industry and a passion about it as well. I learned so much about my personality when I coached with Lisa. I learned that my strengths are advantageous to leadership and play a role in my success.

The network marketing industry has a saying that our business is a personal development program with a compensation plan. Put otherwise, we have to go to work on ourselves before we can go to work with others.

Not only had I already overcome so many self-limiting beliefs and experienced a great deal of personal growth, but I loved it! I recognize how much it impacted my life that I never wanted it to stop. I wanted others to experience that freedom as well. Network marketing became the vehicle to implement so many of my favorite things at once—health and wellness, personal development, and servant leadership.

Ultimately, as I continued to grow my business and experience the benefits of residual income, this opportunity became a platform to do even more. I've always been driven, and I've always wanted to give back, so I started volunteering more, writing more, and speaking more. The more I focused on others, the more doors of opportunity continued to open.

Understanding Myself

By the time I was working with Lisa, I had stepped into high-level leadership, mentoring, and leading more than 10,000 people. Assessments were helping me understand why I did what I did, where I could improve, and also, why others did what they did.

While I may not have been the most popular kid in high school, I was always a leader and influencer. I recall as an early teen always wanting to be at the biggest party where all of the cool kids were. As an adult, I was surrounding myself with shakers, movers, and go-getters. When the marriage of personality tests came together, I could see my true colors.

Understanding all these traits also helped me understand how I can best serve. We are not all motivated the same way. We do not all recognize praise or receive feedback similarly. Coaching with Lisa opened the avenue to communicating with my team uniquely, celebrating and collaborating differently, and most of all, empowering them to find their true colors.

Acceptance Speech

We have all heard the term "imperfectly perfect self" and sayings such as "love yourself just the way you are!" Until you actually do the work yourself, those sayings are more cliché and not as impactful as they are intended to be. One of my favorite exercises with Lisa was developing my acceptance speech, which was the gateway for me to accept myself and love *me*.

None of us are perfect, and no one, to my knowledge, will ever love everything about themselves or not have things they wish they could change, but part of loving ourselves is loving the parts that aren't perfect. To truly love ourselves though, we have to make the choice to accept and love every part of who we are, even our flaws, imperfections, and annoyances.

Think about when you were madly in love with someone, so much so that you adored their quirks, awkward moments, and overlooked their blemishes and shortcomings. Why is it so easy to do that for someone else, but so challenging to do that for ourselves? We can be our own worst critics, and say things to ourselves that we would never say to anyone else, let alone those we care about. We can be so damn cruel to ourselves. That's where the acceptance speech is key.

The acceptance speech includes the things I actually do love about myself and the things I am accepting about myself, but the idea is the conviction is so powerful that someone listening wouldn't be able to decipher which of the statements I did truly love about myself, and which were a part of my positive self-talk and self-love journey.

If someone loved their eyes and wittiness but wished they were taller and didn't like their freckles, the acceptance speech would go something like this: I love my sparkling eyes and I love how quick-witted I am. I love how tall I am and the frequent compliments I get on my freckles.

Can you see how no one would know which features or attributes they really loved about themselves and which ones they wish they could change or alter?

This was so powerful for me that I encourage everyone to do it. I used to read my acceptance speech every morning when I was getting ready, and while I have graduated from that daily practice, I still recite it before a major event, when I am feeling down, during my monthly cycle, or whenever I need a reminder that I am a badass... as are YOU! I don't need to be *perfect* to align with my mission, accomplish my dreams, or manifest my life's vision.

This is my acceptance speech:

I love that I am a go-getter, can accomplish so much at once, and am not a procrastinator.

I love that I am an amazing daughter, sister, friend, leader, and mentor.

I accept my luscious blond locks, my majestic hazel eyes, and my bright white smile.

I am grateful for my strong legs, my fit body, and my athletic shape.

I am thankful to be a powerhouse, a driver, and confident in the decisions I make.

I embrace that I was gifted with the skills of a writer and a speaker and my voice is valuable.

I am beautiful, fun, happy, and living life in the moment.

I am good enough. I am totally accepted. I am lovable, and I am worthy of everything in my life.

How would your acceptance letter read?

RELATIONSHIPS

Family

Shortly before my 34th birthday, I realized how often I was still triggered and started understanding what caused that reaction and how I behaved. I think most, if not all of us, understand the context of truly being triggered, not part of a fake outrage culture, but a true domino effect of emotions that is often connected to a traumatic event. It wasn't until I was coaching with Lisa that I truly understood this process and how to overcome it.

In early June of 2017, an incident occurred that would forever change me. I can recall sitting outside in my stepsister Catherine's backyard in Napa, California, along with her husband Darren and baby boy and my sister Rachael and her husband Jay. I had spoken earlier that day at a conference in San Francisco, and Rach, her husband, and I drove up to Napa afterward to spend time with our other sister and her family.

I remember walking in the door and immediately having a sad feeling, not because I didn't want to be there but because I was the single one. I felt like a fifth wheel. My sister and brother-in-law have a gorgeous home, and I was watching my brother-in-law grill while my sister entertained us with James Taylor quietly playing in the background. I felt teary as I was so envious of their relationship because there was nothing I wanted more than a family. I put on my "big girl" pants, and an even bigger smile, trying to recite my acceptance speech in my head.

During dinner I found myself quiet, doing more listening than talking, which is a rarity for me. I will be the first to admit I can be highly sensitive and take things personally because I care deeply. At the same time, I will also note that I am very intuitive and can often accurately read the energy of a person or a room. One thing I've always said is that while I might not handle my emotions well, I am not triggered without reason... something sets me off.

As we ate dinner, I felt jabs from the sister we were visiting. These may have been unintentional, but given the emotional and mental state I was already in, the comments were bothering me. For example, I had recently put in hair extensions, and she had made a comment, "Why do you have that shit in your hair?"

After dinner, the five of us sat around the fire chatting and drinking wine. Catherine, who had been slightly stressed recently with an infant, missing moments while she was at work, and so forth, was prying (and I felt judging) my involvement, as well as Rachael's involvement, in our network marketing company. While I could feel the tension and the effects of the alcohol, I simply tried to divert the subject. The network marketing company I am in has transformed my life and the lives of countless others, and I am beyond loyal and protective of it. I was hoping that we could transition to a new topic, but that did not happen.

Rachael is a psychologist and often plays the mediator role in the family. She was trying to navigate a conversation between us, but the tone and situation seemed more like a debate than a conversation. All I wanted to do was be unseen, listen to what was happening with others, and be out of the spotlight of attention for the night. Between feeling like no one was in my corner, and frustrated with the way I was being mocked for my involvement in this line of work, I got up to leave. At the time, I intended to just go to the bedroom I would be staying in. I remember this awkward moment, and I stated, "I am leaving..." And the reply I heard was, "That's probably a good idea." That was enough for my story to play, which triggered me to leave ... not just the conversation, but to go home.

I quickly got my belongings and sat outside the house for a ride that could take me back to the San Francisco airport. This was one of the first times *I truly* realized how quickly I could be set off and how a trigger led me to fight or flight (this time flight), but more importantly, I realized how I could create a situation that surely did not benefit me,(actually hurt me) a very familiar feeling.

While I waited for the Uber ride (nearly 45 minutes), I could still hear my family in the backyard. Not one of my four siblings came out to chat with me or encourage me to stay. I was shocked at how well-known this place was to me; the cold, lonely curb. It was freakishly similar to the feeling I always had on Christmas when I was out alone on the curb. As I made the hour-long drive down from Napa in the backseat of an Uber, I cried in a way I have never cried before.

I felt like I hadn't shed tears, especially about my own feelings, in decades, and I poured my eyes out. This trip reminded me of when my dad would take me away from my stepdad's house, the same amount of drive time, and I started realizing how many decades of sadness I had buried, putting on a front, acting as if I didn't care, or trying to be tough when deep inside I was so sad and hurt.

When I got to the airport, which was closed, I remember sitting there in the wee hours of the morning feeling so alone, so sad—and still none of my family reached out to make sure I was OK. While I was feeling hurt and somewhat angry, that was my awakening moment: if things were going to change, it was going to be up to me.

Later that week, in my coaching session with Lisa, I shared with her what had happened. While her heart was sad for me, she broke down my Enneagram personality (8, The Challenger) in a way I will never forget. She explained to me that when I am feeling violated, manipulated, or out of control, my *healing key* is to be vulnerable and to let go. While my instincts are to self-protect, and my default had always been fight or flight, she outlined for me what the other possible scenarios might have been in that situation if I communicated, not self-protected.

As an activator and achiever (StrengthsFinder characteristics), the process of getting triggered and switching into fight-or-flight mode moves at a rapid speed. Sometimes it has happened so quickly I didn't even recognize what upset me. I just felt myself guarding up or shutting down. My brain was always racing, multiple thoughts a second, and I could go down the rabbit hole into a place of self-protecting without even recognizing it, which is what propelled me to fight back or run away.

As Lisa and I worked backward through the events that night, she asked me something so simple but so eye-opening. "What were you *really* feeling and how could things have been different had you articulated that?" As I reflect back to my arrival at my sister's house, I could've shared with my sisters that I was so happy for them but hurting inside that I was 34, still single, and still no kids. I am sure they would've immediately been empathetic; however, they didn't know I buried that feeling. If you remember, I was constantly on this path of being good enough, so for me to share that I was sad made me feel weak, not good enough, and broken instead of feeling empowered to be vulnerable and transparent.

As I reflect back on the evening, I did not take the blame for it all, but for the first time, I realized that if I had communicated differently, the outcome could've been significantly different. I understood that the way I conditioned myself to self-protect was further isolating me from people, fueling my innate distrust for people, and affirming a story that wasn't true, even if I had become accustomed to it.

Understanding this dynamic helps me in all my relationships, especially when it comes to romance. Being vulnerable is not easy for me, and it surely isn't my first nature. Although, understanding myself definitely changed me from always self-protecting and wanting to escape, to actually becoming closer, allowing others in, and ultimately, trusting.

Romantic Relationships

I am the type of person who can meet someone in line at the grocery store and be best friends by the end of the week. Everywhere I go, I talk to people, meet people, and make new friends. Whether it's sitting at a restaurant bar, on a plane, or even a spin bike in a class, finding and making friends has always come easy to me. However, finding a quality romantic relationship or *keeping* one was a completely different story and actually was a constant battle.

In my heart, and in my mind, I knew exactly what I wanted. I couldn't see exact details of what he would look like or how he would dress, but I could see the perfect relationship for me. I could visualize the relationship where we worked out together, cooked together, took on chores and responsibilities together, and could enjoy all of life's activities together. It was easy for me to see myself on the couch watching football and eating banana pancakes with my love or getting dressed up and hitting the town together for wine and tapas. I could envision hosting family events and holidays together, traveling the world, and raising a family with someone, but sadly, the relationship cards weren't falling into place. What seemed so easy to see was so hard to bring to fruition.

For the longest time, I allowed the story of *I'll never find a good guy* or *All the good men are taken* to play over and over again in my head. My friends and family assured me I would find the right man, and that I deserved someone wonderful. In the meantime, I kept finding bad relationship after bad relationship, which only perpetuated the story in my mind.

I remember telling a good friend a story about a guy I was dating at the time. I remember telling her how I felt like I was hidden, being kept a secret. I remember explaining to her I felt like we were *good* in private, but with friends or co-workers around, it felt like he didn't want anyone to know we were a couple. It was as if he was ashamed of me. I remember telling her I felt like he was interested in other women

I wasn't enough for him, but then she said something to me I'll never forget. Have you ever had someone who cares about you give a piece of advice that just lands—it shakes you to your core? This was that type of statement.

She explained to me that I have a high pain tolerance. Because I experienced so much hurt and exploitation in my past, when things hurt or don't feel right but are not "bad enough," I almost dismiss them. She elaborated that since my current level of pain wasn't as high as other times of shame, hurt, or rejection I've experienced, I didn't see it as *that bad* or unhealthy compared to what I experienced in the past. I remember her rolling her shoulders back, lifting her chest, and looking at me dead in the eyes and saying, "Lauren, *no one* should hurt you. It doesn't matter if it is a little bit or a lot of pain, *no one* who loves you would intentionally hurt you."

I sat at the coffee shop, tears rolling down my face, reflecting on all of the men I had dated, all of the men who disrespected me or had taken advantage of me because I didn't have standards for myself. I was the enabler of sleazeballs and dirtbags. I was the one who chose to tolerate it. It was my reflection I needed to face in the mirror about what I was allowing. I could no longer point the finger and blame other people. The only actions we can control are our own. I wasn't going to change these men, so if I wanted the relationship status to change, *I* had to change.

Sometimes it's easier to put the accusation or complaint onto someone else, but at the end of the day, we get to choose what we deserve, who merits space in our lives, and what we will tolerate. I'm not sure my belief that I would find a loving and patient man skyrocketed right at that moment, but I confidently did draw a line in the sand of what I would no longer abide or accept as I *knew* there had to be something more.

In addition to being a bad picker, I always seemed to push away the good boys or sabotage those relationships. Had I become so addicted to the highs and lows; the rollercoaster of emotions with unstable relationships that I questioned the good ones? The lack of drama, or the chase, or proving I was good enough, made me ask, *Is this love?* The security and stability, even though it was what I wanted, almost represented boredom to me, and I would nitpick situations, almost subconsciously, testing how someone would respond or react. *Would this one fight for me?*

Have you ever noticed yourself finding problems in areas that actually don't have problems? I didn't realize at the time that I wasn't open to nice men or that I was subconsciously finding imperfections in ways that caused me to overlook their qualities, simply because I was afraid to get hurt. Somewhere in my brain, and in my heart, I didn't believe I was lovable and deserving. I was so afraid to be let down that I didn't let my guard down. I was afraid to end up alone again... in my familiar spot on the curb of life.

I already knew what it felt like to be disappointed by people I cared about, to have someone not respect me, or even worse, disrespect me. Somehow, I gravitated to these unhealthy relationships because even though I knew they weren't going to work, I was familiar with how they felt. That feeling of control and familiarity about the outcome kept me in a broken cycle.

After being on a personal growth and personal development journey, I now look back and realize that subconsciously I did not believe I was worthy or deserving of a good relationship. It's almost as if I was addicted to the drama or was comfortable in bad relationships, even if it wasn't serving me in a positive way. A deep-rooted story said that if my own family didn't love me and protect me, how could a man unconditionally love me and protect me?

The irony was that I had so many friends I could trust wholeheartedly, but when it came to a relationship, the expectations I put on them were unrealistic and incongruent with the platonic relationships in my life. I didn't realize there was such an emptiness in my heart, such a big void of love, that it was next to impossible for any one person to fill or fix that void. No matter what someone did, it was never enough. After decades of blaming someone else, I finally realized that the only person who could fill that emptiness was me.

It took years of personal development and loving myself from within before I could open my heart to a healthy relationship. I learned a relationship was going to balance me and better me, but it wasn't capable of completing me. I realized a relationship was going to enhance my life, not fill an area of unfinished business.

****

I look back and I think of times when I was disappointed or frustrated by someone I was dating, and it's because I either had an unrealistic expectation of them or a brokenness inside of me, neither of which was their responsibility to fix. Some days I was sad that I wasn't making the money I thought I deserved, frustrated with my weight, or didn't like the person I was. Without realizing it, I was taking my frustrations and stress out on them. I also didn't really know how I wanted someone to express love to me, so sometimes a kind action could be done, but I was expecting it to look different, so I found myself disappointed and frustrated.

When you are in that frame of mind, no one can fix it but yourself. Kind words, compliments, and hugs make you feel better for a moment, but ultimately, that core issue, your definition of happiness, can only be found within and not be fulfilled from the outside. Tony Robbins has a saying about trading expectation for appreciation, and I noticed all of my relationships, not just romantic, began to shift for the better when I let go of an expected outcome and focused on gratitude for what value or experiences that person gave me.

Even today, instead of ever highlighting what someone hasn't done, I choose to spotlight everything they do. Maybe the dishwasher wasn't unloaded, but maybe the bed was made. Which do you want to focus on? Maybe the flowers weren't sent on your birthday, but you always find love notes around the house for you. Trading expectation for appreciation was a game changer for me.

Self-Sabotage

When it came to self-sabotage, I used to be the queen bee! I was the girl who could get herself out of $15,000 to $20,000 in credit card debt only to end up right back in the same situation in a matter of weeks. I was the girl who would lose 10 to15 pounds through dieting and overtraining, and then binge eat until I gained 20 pounds again. I habitually did things, often subconsciously, that kept me in a place that was uncomfortable, limiting, and not beneficial at all.

An area where I *habitually* did this was in relationships. My communication skills were already less than par and I was also easily triggered. I shifted into my familiar place of fight or flight, and I often found myself sitting alone waiting to be rescued from my self-inflicted devastation.

After years of childhood ridicule, losing my best friend, and being lied to and cheated on numerous times, I didn't innately trust that people had good intentions, especially since I was still wrestling with my overly sensitive personality and heart. What

I learned later, after working with my life coach, was that I was afraid of being vulnerable or being out of control. If I felt I could be hurt or out of control, I would either shut down or guard up.

Not only was this so challenging and frustrating for me, but you can imagine how this was received on the other end. It's natural to gently tease our loved ones sometimes. At times I wouldn't feel it in a lovingly way and literally snap. How could someone know when it was an appropriate time to tease me and when I would freak out? When I stopped playing a victim and chose to do the work, my relationships started to change.

****

I may not have actually been isolated on a street curb, but metaphorically, it was a place I knew so well. It had been terrible, lonely, scary and frequently resurfaced time and time again in my life. I would fall hard, and breakups hit me even harder. When I *fought* with a partner, I never felt that I was supported or my feelings were justified, which left such a lonely piece in my heart.

I didn't know it at the time, but looking back, I was constantly 'self-protecting.' If the slightest comment, remark, or situation made me feel violated or manipulated, or if anything was untrusting, I could go 0 to 60 faster than any race car in how I guarded up. I recognize this not only happened with my romantic relationships, but also with close family relationships that I knew were unconditional, such as my sister.

Sometimes we want something so badly that we compromise our values. I was so tired of finding emotionally unavailable men, and one day I thought, *How could someone open up to me, when I am emotionally unavailable?* What I wanted so badly was never going to happen if I continued to defend, protect, and sabotage myself.

Then

I have done my share of dating, but have not had many serious relationships, because each of them was significant in length. I have lived with two of my boyfriends, and one was a terrible experience. My college boyfriend Duncan and I got along fine, so I know I am capable of cohabitating; however, the last serious relationship I had in my late 20s, with Brooks, was not a positive living experience.

Brooks and I had been together for a couple of years, so living together seemed like the natural next step. This man was really not the type to trust, let anyone into his space, or compromise. In fact, the move led to the demise of our relationship. Brooks was raised in Compton where a lot of people close to him abandoned him, which led to major trust issues. His brother was involved in gang activity. His father was never in the picture, so he learned early on that putting himself first and doing what was best for him was how he was going to get through life.

When it came to living together, everything was very separate. Nothing felt like ours, and his control over the space made life beyond uncomfortable. Even though I felt like I was walking on eggshells, wondering if I used the right sponge to wipe down the granite countertops, making sure the coffee maker didn't wake him or hoping I hung my wet towel in the right place that wouldn't affect the paint on the bathroom door, I was somehow OK with this control.

I've heard the saying over and over that we often stay in situations that are comfortable, even if they don't serve us, simply because they are familiar. As a young kid, back in my mom and stepdad's house, it's almost as if I learned that home is a place of discomfort, it's normal to have anxiety and fear of upsetting others in the home... especially the man of the house.

In addition to Brooks being incredibly particular and distrusting, I didn't have the password to our garage or access to the iPad, and everything he did was secretive. To add to the discomfort, I was the one who moved in with him. We didn't go into a place together; rather, I left my space and tried to merge into his.

When I moved out of my condo, I got rid of most of my belongings. He had nicer, newer items at the time, and we surely didn't need two of everything. When we broke up, it was abrupt, and I was the one looking for a new place, repurchasing furniture, and resetting my life. Again! The move out reminded me of the curb, a lonely place where I couldn't help but ask, *Why am I not enough?* That level of distrust and disruption did prepare me more for the next relationship: The Liar.

Brooks and I spent years together (on and off), and while we had fun and we got along, our long-term visions and core values did not ever sync up. When we broke up, shortly after my 30th birthday, I vowed not to get into a relationship unless it had long-term potential for two reasons. One was that I had really wanted to get clear on my core values, and what mattered most. Two, I wanted to enjoy the single life, since I had spent more time in relationships than alone.

Even though the relationships weren't stellar, I spent much of young adulthood with someone else, and wanted some *me* time! I didn't want to spend time with someone unless I thought there was a future. I was getting older, my dad was getting sicker, my baby-making clock was ticking, and I knew time is valuable... any time I spend with someone that wasn't leading me to happily ever after was time I wasn't going to get back.

When you are in your 20s, often you date for fun and companionship, but as you get older, if marriage and kids are important, your focus changes. After a few good years in my 30s of being single, only having to worry about myself, enjoying lots of girls' nights out, and experiencing my share of swiping left and right with online dating apps, I met a man, Edward, when I least expected it. He *appeared* to be everything I was searching and waiting for.

On first impression, Edward was not only attractive (there was initial chemistry), but he elevated me in a way I never experienced before. I had this unique sense of him just understanding me for me in a way I had never felt before. After two wonderful dates he returned home to his state, as he had only been in my town temporarily for work. We built an amazing friendship over the next few months, talked daily, shared our deepest and darkest secrets with each other, and I found an excitement, an attraction, and an openness I hadn't felt in a long time.

It was interesting how I didn't seem to find real chemistry or a solid connection with so many men I had been on dates with in my home city of Denver and, suddenly, a man far away had my full attention. In addition to consistent good morning and goodnight texts, which was a *win* for me, here was someone who seemed to be genuinely taking an interest in my life, cheering me on, and excited for me or proud of me.

These were foreign feelings, and I latched on like crazy! It has been so long since I felt *enough* (in a relationship) and pursued, that it blinded me. I would be lying if I didn't also share that something felt off, or too good to be true, but I often ignored it, I wanted *love* so badly. I would sometimes share my sixth sense, intuitive feeling with my girlfriends, and they dismissed it, told me I was sabotaging something wonderful, and not to overstress.

After months of messaging and talking on the phone, we decided to meet again, to see if we actually had something special here. Even though we only spent two days in person, t we felt a closeness as if we'd known each other our whole lives. As we counted down the days to get together, it felt like Christmas was coming.

I remember doing everything just right to get ready for our trip. We were going to meet in a neutral location, not either of our hometowns, and I couldn't wait! I got a haircut, a spray tan, a manicure and pedicure, bought new clothes, and was ready to put on my best version of myself to win over the man I thought was my real-life Prince Charming. I arrived in St. Louis, the city where we decided to meet, and after months of anticipation to see each other, the meeting was anything but fairytale material.

Almost immediately after reuniting there was an incredible disconnect, a sense of anxiousness or tension, not nerves. I knew something very fishy was going on. Without even spending 24 hours together, he got a call that his grandma was in the hospital. He told me they didn't think she was going to make it through the night, and he had to rush home.

I *knew* with 100 percent certainty that nothing was wrong with his grandma, and I also knew something was completely wrong with *us* and was determined to get to the bottom of it. After sending a text message basically demanding the truth if we were ever going to speak again and promising forgiveness, as long as I got the truth, I did receive an absolute truth bomb.

Unbeknownst to me, he was apparently unhappy in an 11-year relationship with four kids, three of whom were not his biological kids. While I was so hurt and felt so betrayed, thinking, *I have been so vulnerable to him the last few months, and I have fallen for someone who doesn't even exist.*

I fell for his sob story about how poorly he was treated, how he selfishly needed love and didn't mean to lead me on, blah, blah, blah. In addition to being in my mid-30s, and wanting to be married and start a family so badly, my dad's health was declining quickly. I think I speak for all girls who are close to their dads when I say our biggest dream is to have Dad walk us down the aisle.

The pressure was on for me, not from my dad, but from myself. All three of my older sisters were married, had already experienced the father-daughter dance, and I wanted it. Instead of walking away from this relationship immediately, and seeing a liar, a cheater, and a manipulator, I focused on our chemistry, believed his story that he was going to leave his partner for me, and justified that I didn't *know* all of this before I fell for him and somehow that made it right.

I wanted certain things so badly I told myself, "Everything happens for a reason," that we don't meet people by accident, and compromised my integrity. I tried forcing my dream vision into the most unhealthy and incongruent relationship I had ever been in.

If I *knew* that an abundance of wonderful men was out there, and if I *knew* that I was worthy and deserving of an incredible relationship, I would've walked away; however, what I know now, and did not know or see then, was that I was still so broken inside. My belief in how I deserved to be treated was so low that

I settled, would've done anything to make it work, because, *This was as good as it was going to get...* for me.

Choose Your Lens

The super-toxic relationship before the love of my life showed up allowed me to experience agony and rejection in a way I didn't even know was possible. I faced the reality that I was in a relationship that not only didn't serve me but was also actually hurting me and everyone else involved.

I had a vision of taking my dad and stepmom to Tahiti with me and The Liar, as well as my sisters and their husbands. My dad was such a giver to us all and it was a bucket list vacation place for him. I had a dream that we could take him as a retirement gift before the Parkinson's disease took over. I worked on this goal for more than two years, and right when this relationship was coming to an end, I realized my goal was a dream that might not come true.

What I was experiencing was not the celebration of planning this family destination, but rather the familiar feeling of being left on the curb. Mine and Edward's breakup was occurring at the same time as this planning. While the focus should have been on my dad, my heart only felt, *Everyone has someone to go with except me... you're still alone, Lauren.*

I will be the first to recognize that it was not the relationship I wanted, but even under those circumstances, instead of feeling in control, having self-worth, and wanting more, my underlying feeling was, *I was not worth fighting for...* I wanted so badly for it all to have worked out, all of the tears, time, travel, and betrayal to have been for something. The reality was that not only did that man never leave his life partner and family (thank goodness!), but my dad's health was simultaneously declining. I was putting a lot of pressure on myself with life's "clocks" and found myself isolated, unhappy, and even incongruent with my core values.

I reached out to my dear friend and life coach, Lisa, who reminded me of the lens of joy and the lens of judgment. When we come from judgment, we are shameful, powerless, hopeless, blaming, and feel as though nothing can change. When we come from joy, we are shameless, powerful, and hopeful, take action, and believe life can always change.

It's fair to say that today most people would describe me as positive, driven, ambitious, and confident, but on the inside, I face the same challenges, experience the same conflicts, and undergo the same pressure as everyone else. When this relationship came to an end, I took back the voice I had lost and made a decision: *If it is going to be, it is up to me!*

I couldn't wait for someone else to get their ducks in a row so my dreams could come true. I knew the *right* man for me was going to choose me, not juggle me with anyone else, and wouldn't have me as second place or a backup plan.

One day at a time, I focused on new goals, took initiative toward new dreams, stopped blaming myself, and most of all believed that everything happens for a reason and is always preparing me for what's next. I knew this experience and these choices were for a reason. I didn't stay in a place of regret because I couldn't go back and do things differently. Instead, I took the pain and frustration and let that fuel me to get stronger, clearer, and more aligned with what I really wanted, and not what I was trying to fix or force.

I was on a morning run with Whitney Houston pouring into my ears, and I found myself in my truth—full of purpose, passion, and gratitude. With a huge smile on my face, I gained clarity of what was next. I let go of expectations that didn't serve me and my heart reminded me of a message I want to share with you right now: *tough times don't last, but tough people do.*

Little reminders pop up in life to keep me seeing through the lens of joy. This is the lens I want to share with you today: choose joy. You are powerful. You are the creator of your future. Things can always change. Surprise yourself. You never know where just ONE decision will lead you.

If you take anything away from this, it is to treat yourself the way you want to be treated and stop waiting for someone else to do it! Be the person you want to attract. If you don't want people to be rude to you, don't be rude to them. If you don't want someone unhealthy or unfit then be healthy and fit.

Stop justifying and compromising because the only person you are hurting is you. When you recognize who you are, what you deserve, and how you should be treated, you not only won't settle, but you also won't tolerate any bullshit along the way.

Lastly, be the person you want to attract! I was so tired of finding emotionally unavailable men and one day I realized, *How could someone open up to me when I am emotionally unavailable?* What I wanted so badly was never going to happen if I continued to defend, protect, and sabotage myself.

Now

I am in a relationship now, that is *the one*, the one that showed up when I least expected it, when I wasn't trying, in a way different than I anticipated, when I was ready for it. This is the one that ignites every cell of my body that this is the person created for me.

The love of my life is Ryan, and while he is perfect for me, in the beginning we had some growing pains simply because of my guarded heart and the hurt of the past. When we first started dating, Ryan was building a brand-new home. Within a couple of weeks of seeing each other, he showed me the model and actually asked me to attend the design sessions. I remember thinking, *Is this guy nuts? We've just barely met!* And simultaneously thinking, *Wow, he wants my opinion?* Ryan mentioned he saw me living there, but at the time, I really didn't. I was going more as a supportive friend, trying to offer the feminine eye.

We spent hours of discussions over cabinet colors, the type of grout for the shower floor, and what style of carpet and hardwood floors may look best, and I was detached from the idea I would be living there. Even though I wanted it, I didn't believe the happily ever after story was going to happen to me.

A few months passed, and his mom was in town visiting. Ryan wanted to take her to the model home as she hadn't seen it yet. I happened to be with him and went along. From the time period of the last design session to our second visit to the model home, a lot had changed between us in regards to the closeness and seriousness of our relationship. We had talked about moving in together, even dreaming big about hosting Thanksgiving together, but we didn't have many conversations about the day-to-day challenges it might present.

As we toured the home, I could feel a trigger coming on. While Ryan was excitedly showing his mom different parts of the home, I suddenly was panicking that there wasn't an office for me, a place for me to work. I am self-employed and couldn't see myself working from there. I started having flashbacks of the fights with Brooks and suddenly was less excited at the idea of moving in. I was instantly anxious about moving into another man's house.

Even though it was a brand-new home, and no one had lived in it, we didn't pick it out together. We didn't shop for neighborhoods together, and ultimately, if something went wrong, I would be the one moving out, back to square one, and once again rebuilding. I literally could feel the similarities. Instead of trusting that this man was so kind and inclusive, I found myself fearing the worst and retracting into my shell.

I was too afraid to get hurt, too afraid to wind up alone. I wasn't allowing myself to get excited about the possibilities, about what felt like a real-life dream come true. Have you ever experienced something like this? The only limitation in this situation was me.

We got in the car and I was quiet, shut down, distant, and my nonverbal body language said enough. When I self-protect and guard up, most people can feel my shift. Ryan immediately asked me what was wrong, and if I was OK. All he got was a lot of "I'm fine," and "I'm good," which was clearly not the truth. What I know is that those fears or concerns are legitimate, but my inability to effectively communicate, be vulnerable, and share my feelings was not OK.

I *know* with certainty that if I had told Ryan we needed to chat and had opened up to him, he would have been supportive, empathetic, and compassionate. Unfortunately, this vicious fight-or-flight cycle kicks in so fast, almost automatically, that I often need to work backward to recognize the trigger and then articulate the emotions. It's a response that happens, and then, I logically and consciously have to interpret and analyze my reaction before I can discuss it. In the past, I wouldn't have felt *safe* enough to have the conversation; however, with Ryan, not only am I *finally* able to effectively communicate and be vulnerable but he also "gets me." At 35 years old I am no longer misunderstood! Hallelujah!

THE FOUR AGREEMENTS

In his book *The Four Agreements*, author Don Miguel Ruiz gives four principles to reveal the source of many self-limiting beliefs and how these principles create love and happiness in your life when put into practice.

Do yourself a favor and go buy *The Four Agreements*. The concepts are not complex, and in my opinion, when adopted into daily living, they can be extremely transformative and life-giving.

The Four Agreements are:

1. Be Impeccable With Your Word
2. Don't Take Anything Personally
3. Don't Make Assumptions
4. Always Do Your Best

After countless hours of coaching, counseling, and personal development, I learned that life will never be perfect. We will always face challenges, and we can't control the actions of others, only how we respond or react to the situation. When I think of these four agreements, I think about how I apply them daily in my own life, with those I coach, and as I continue to work through areas of my past.

Be Impeccable with your Word

For some people, this may seem as simple as being honest or having integrity, but to me, it is so much more. Our words are reflections of how we feel about ourselves and others. Communication is essential to healthy relationships with ourselves and with others. We're all familiar with the Golden Rule, treating others how you would like to be treated, and in my opinion, this starts with the words coming out of our mouths.

After being the casualty of someone else's harsh words, I am so cognizant of how I speak about others. As the old adage goes, if you don't have anything nice to say, don't say it at all. I am surely not the one to look the other way and not to stand up for something I believe in—c'mon, I am the Challenger! However, I make a conscious effort not to gossip or put others down in order to elevate myself and to follow through and have integrity with what I say.

Many of us recognize we do not shine by putting others down, and we rise by lifting others up, but why do you think so many of us are so two-faced? So quick to make crude comments to one another, or even worse, behind someone's back? I know that for me it was because I felt so small inside; that's the only way I knew how to feel big, but today gossip makes me cringe. Catty comments infuriate me. Embellishing and over exaggerating is unnecessary, and not only is it dishonest, but it often intimidates others. Sometimes the truth hurts, but I truly believe it is always the best policy, so even when we make mistakes, we can be honest because dishonesty and deceitfulness never win. I am an advocate of: if you say you are going to do something, do it! I am a firm believer that actions speak louder than words, so if you commit, follow through.

Lastly, here's a tip of advice: believe what people show you, not what they tell you. In my business I hear a lot of talk but often see no action. Many of us can talk a big game, but taking action on those words is what matters most. One last thing. Pay attention to how you speak to yourself. Sometimes we are our own worst critics, and we say the most critical and harsh things to ourselves. If we don't say loving things to ourselves, how can we expect better words from anyone else? "I am" statements are real and they work when you are on a journey of loving yourself, so get clear on who you are and start reciting those instead of subscribing to the constant reel of negative self-talk you may have on repeat.

So, who are you? I am certain that when we are at peace with ourselves, we not only let go of judgment of others, but we also are able to step into the best version of ourselves. Here are some of my I AM messages. I encourage you to get clear on who you are and every day strive to be a little better and grow a little more.

I am ...
- A leader
- A fit and healthy young woman
- A strong and independent woman of change
- An amazing daughter, sister, and significant other
- Honest, loyal, supportive, and forgiving
- Getting better and growing more every day.

The statements will be different for everyone, but just as athletes practice every day, we have to take action every day to fuel our minds with what we want and not what we don't want. Showing up as a person full of truth and love starts with you.

Don't Take Anything Personally

One of the most challenging lessons I've learned is that nothing other people do is because of me. Instead, it is a projection of their own reality, issues, and frustrations. It's so easy to get lost in a story that often has nothing to do with us. Have you ever walked into a party and someone is in a bad mood or not overly friendly? Without even thinking about it, we tell ourselves they don't like us or judge them on their behavior without even considering what else could be going on in their life.

I attended a seminar where I heard Robin Sharma describe a metaphorical shirt that influencers wear. On the front it says *Leader* and on the back it says *Target*.

His point was that it's easy to accept the praise, but how do you respond to those who don't support what you're doing? As monumental and impactful as Martin Luther King, Jr., was, imagine if he had listened to the naysayers, the haters, and the racists? His vision was too strong to internalize what other people were saying, but not all of us are as strong as Dr. King.

Another great book I read is *What You Think Of Me Is None Of My Business* by Terry Cole-Whittaker. As someone with a very sensitive heart, I was consistently caught up in drama! I wanted everyone to like me. I wanted to make everyone happy, but at the end of the day, you can't please everyone. For those you can't make happy, you can't spend time worrying about it.

I'm certainly not advocating a my-way-or-the-highway mentality, but rather, give yourself permission to not take ownership of other people's opinions, thoughts, actions, or behaviors. As a leader, I will have team members call and say "Lauren, you did this..." or "Lauren, you didn't do this..." While I patiently listen, sometimes I need to recognize I'm not actually the problem, but rather the target of blame or a projection of frustration when others aren't taking ownership of their own choices.

When I look back at my early teen years, I'm not sure if I was able to not take things personally. Today though, as a self-loving, confident, and successful woman, I don't. Even in the most present times, someone can say things I find offensive, but I *choose* to put a shield up around my heart, not to be defensive but instead know that I can't control what others say or do. If I take it personally, the only person who suffers is me.

We might not always like how someone speaks to us or we might not feel good about how someone behaves, but remember, personalizing someone else's behavior only makes matters worse for you. Building up an immunity to the opinions and actions of others will protect you from falling victim to needless suffering.

Don't Make Assumptions

I wish in school I could have had fewer algebra lessons and science experiments and more communication and relationship classes. Granted, I went through some major life experiences that led me to a conditioned response of fight or flight, but I have also reflected back and thought, *What if I had just had the courage to ask questions of someone's intentions or been able to more clearly state what I wanted or how I was feeling? How would things have been different?*

On a daily basis when I work with my team or in my relationships (friends, family, and boyfriend), I commit not to assume or defensively self-protect but to seek clarity so we can avoid any unnecessary drama, misunderstandings, or avoidable heartache. It is such an easy pattern for many of us to slip into. It's best to take the extra moment to hash out the uncertainty instead of concluding and making your own assumptions.

Think about how often you jump to conclusions. Maybe someone wasn't where they said they were going to be. Maybe someone didn't call you back. For those of you in sales, have you ever felt rejected or unclear on the unfavorable outcome of the transaction? For those of you with kids, have you ever assumed something and later found out that wasn't the case? The key to this is giving people the benefit of the doubt in addition to taking a moment to ask clarifying questions. When we make assumptions we react. When we ask questions we give ourselves time to respond.

Always Do Your Best

The most difficult areas of leadership for me are letting go of the idea that I can please everyone and that everyone will like me. I heard at a seminar once that 20 percent will always love you, 20 percent will always dislike you, and 60 percent will be fair-weather fans. When I started to think about ministers, politicians, sports teams, or even celebrities, I started to see how accurate this was.

Under any circumstance, it is impossible to win everyone over or meet the expectations of everyone. This is why it is crucial to set your own standards, and then do your best to meet or exceed them. In the past I would lead team conference calls, and after hanging up, criticize myself about how I disappointed everyone or didn't provide enough value. Frequently, after teaching a group fitness class, I was upset that not everyone seemed pleased, or was concerned that certain members didn't love the playlist I chose, as opposed to feeling grateful for my health, the workout, or the positive experience I created for most of the class.

I think there is a massive difference between cutting corners to get things done and over-criticizing ourselves. I used to procrastinate with homework and at the last minute would try to rush the project. I can hear my dad's voice today, "A job not done well is a job not worth doing at all." I can recall as a kid when I would hurry to clean my room, my mom would find all of my clothes shoved underneath the bed, or everything crammed into the closet. What could have been done once the right way always took me so much longer, having to do over a second time. Fortunately as I matured, I learned the value of hard work, found pride in my work ethic, and have distanced myself from these formerly poor habits; however, I can still put too much pressure on myself, even when I have put in the proper amount of time and effort into a task.

Have you ever heard the saying from Teddy Roosevelt, "Comparison is the thief of joy?" While I know I am anything but a slacker, I can often find myself wrapped up in what someone else is doing better, or consumed with worrying about someone else's trajectory. In fitness, I compared who ran faster or who lifted heavier. In my network marketing business, it might be who is advancing to the next rank quicker. With my personal relationships, I used to find myself comparing events or life situations.

Can you relate? These thoughts create so much stress in life, and ultimately they'll keep you from so much happiness and fulfillment. It's that simple. If you are half-assing things, and you know you can do better, then stop putzing around and do better.

If at the end of the day you can look yourself in the mirror and know that you gave it your all—no matter what it is—then that is what ultimately matters. You did the best you could. We are all going to have good days and bad days and areas we excel in more than others, so remember, doing your best is *your* best and no one else's.

Never Take Anything For Granted

The four agreements was a pivotal read, and I've been applying the agreements to my life and paying them forward ever since. I also abide by a fifth agreement, one that is not discussed in the book, but rather my own that I apply to my life. Agreement number five is to never take anything for granted.

We hear things such as "tomorrow is not promised" or asked tough questions such as, "What if you could no longer hear or see, or what if you were born deaf or blind?" These are supposed to help us create perspective for everything we have.

What if we woke up tomorrow with only what we were grateful for today? What would we have left? It is so easy to get worked up, annoyed and frustrated in our daily lives, but I highly encourage you not to focus on problems or complaints. You will only attract in more of those things, and you will dilute the positives and the daily celebrations. When we complain about strain or pain, we limit ourselves from possibility, growth, and change. Additionally, negativity is contagious; we give it to others, as opposed to spreading light and love.

To change your perspective, when you complain about your job, think about someone who just lost theirs, or doesn't have one. I think about times I can get frustrated with my mom when I am "too busy," and remind myself of someone who doesn't have a mom. Sometimes when I complain there isn't the right food in the house, or nothing sounds good, I think of everyone in the world who is hungry, who doesn't have anything at all to eat, and I suddenly find myself much less picky. I encourage you to go one day, just 24 hours without complaining and see how your life changes. I once heard Jay Shetty say, "The secret to having it all is knowing you already do."

This message first hit home with me when Mary was murdered. I wouldn't say I took our friendship for granted, but I didn't believe something could ever happen, and therefore never had a chance to tell her what she meant to me. As I got older, I witnessed friend's parents have sudden heart attacks, and friends who were significantly hurt in car accidents, and I have known too many people diagnosed with cancer.

Additionally, I've seen people go through tremendous struggles with sudden job layoffs, marital affairs, or financial emergencies. I bring all of this up because worrying about the past or worrying about the future prevents us from being in the now. Every day we have blessings. Every day we are given gifts: the fact that you get out of bed and your feet work and you walk; the fact that you have a job and receive a paycheck; the fact that you have a significant other or friends and family to come home to.

One thing that helps me when I get irritated, or frustrated, is to return to gratitude. Sometimes when we are focused on what we don't have, we forget everything we do.

In my mid-20s, when I was teaching group fitness classes 15 to 20 hours a week and I was in phenomenal shape, competing in fitness shows, doing triathlons, and personal training, I hurt my back. I was taking CrossFit classes and allowed my competitive nature to push me beyond my limits. Instead of resting and taking time off, I kept pushing because I needed the income, and have a very hard time not exercising.

The consequence of not listening to my body, and continuing to push, was two bulging discs and two herniated discs. Anyone with back pain knows how excruciating this is, and for those of you who don't, I will sum it up with this... barely able to walk, unable to drive, unable to sit, unable to stand, minimal positions lying down were possible, all filled with shooting pain down my legs. I had to use the restroom standing up, was not able to work, and clearly could not exercise.

I was in my 20s, and I assure you I never thought I would be on disability, especially as a young and fit individual. After months of rehab, physical therapy, and chiropractic care, I nursed myself back to health; however, more than 10 years later, I still move gingerly with some activities, am cautious with physical demands, and appreciate the health of my physical body more than ever. Sometimes we don't realize what we have until we lose it, and I vowed to myself that I would do my best to not take things for granted. We all know that complaining about yesterday won't make tomorrow any better.

I can make tomorrow better in a few ways: First, I don't leave friends or family in the midst of arguments. Secondly, I don't go to the gym to beat up my body, or out train cookies and ice cream, but rather with gratitude that I am able to and I choose to exercise. Most of all, I tell people I love them when I can and enjoy each day because someday it will be the last one.

I rise with intention, purpose, and gratitude, and I go to bed with love, fulfillment and again... gratitude. I wake up asking myself, *What can I do to be one percent better than yesterday?* And, *What is something right now I can do that will bring me joy?* A question I ask myself every night, and anyone who happens to be around me that night, whether it is my boyfriend, a friend, or family members, is, "What was the best part of your day today"? That is the last thing I think about.

****

If today was the last day of your life, how would it impact the way you think? If today was the last day of your life, how would you change the way you talk to people? If today was the last day of your life, would you behave differently? I don't mean go skydiving or bungee jumping, but rather embrace everything you have already been given? Would your interactions or communication be different knowing the last thing you said would be the last time that person ever heard your voice?

Be mindful of what you say today, because you may not have tomorrow to take it back.

THE INFLUENCERS WHO HELPED MAKE ME WHO I AM TODAY

It's easy to see the *glory* without always knowing the *story*. Sometimes we look up to people, even envy people, without knowing their experiences, challenges, obstacles, or opportunities.

I remember my first time speaking onstage for my network marketing company. So many attendees said to me, "Lauren, you *have* to share your story." At the time, I thought they wanted my rags-to-riches network marketing story. As time went on and I continued to do the work on myself, I realized I had a much bigger story to tell.

People from my high school probably still don't know I graduated early. There's a good chance they probably think I was a high school dropout since I never came back after winter break. Former boyfriends out there probably believe I'm too high maintenance or cause too much drama to marry. Team members, clients, and friends probably see a strong, independent, confident, and successful woman and have no idea about everything I've been through.

Most importantly, many people in my life know my rough beginnings. They've seen the turnaround but don't necessarily understand all that's transpired. This story is part of my behind-the-curtain conversation to explain what happened.

As success came into my life, everyone wanted to know *how* I did it, but the older I get, I realize we have no true arrival point of success, because we need to be always growing, evolving, learning, and inevitably, changing. The *how* is always changing. When I think about what I did, or what I do, it's impossible to share without giving credit to amazing leaders, speakers, coaches, and mentors who paved the way.

Tony

I started following Tony Robbins about 10 years ago. I can remember watching his YouTube videos that popped up on Facebook. I know where I was standing when I started downloading his podcasts. I'll never forget how I felt when I first read *Awakening the Giant Within*. Tony captured my attention— his story resonated with me for so many reasons.

Not only is he positive, motivational, encouraging, engaging, and wise, but he also comes from hardship. I quickly realized that part of why he was so compassionate, empathetic, and skilled at shifting people. It's because he went first. He already did the work to recover and then he started inspiring and educating others.

Tony grew up in a very abusive home. He often went to bed hungry and left home at 17. He never pursued a formal education and went on to be a world-renowned speaker and one of the most influential people in the world. I've heard Tony speak at various conferences and also attended his *Unleash the Power Within* experience, and yes, I am a fire walker.

I've always been inspired by his success, but mostly his grit, determination, and obsession with growth and contribution. One of Tony's famous quotes is "Repetition is the mother of all skill." Simply put, we learn and improve by doing things over and over again. When you look at famous athletes, such as elite basketball player LeBron James, or world-class golfer Tiger Woods; they are both still practicing.

When it comes to ourselves though, sometimes we don't maintain the same standard. I know I'm not alone when I say that I read a self-help book or attend a personal development conference, and suddenly, I feel unstoppable and bulletproof only to slide back into old habits and behaviors days or weeks later.

****

Working on our mindset or choosing a state to operate in is not a one-time decision. It is a constant decision that requires daily commitment and dedication. Just as athletes continue to show up for practice, we have to continue to show up as our best selves by consciously choosing to get better.

It's simple: are you spending more time feeding your brain things that will get you closer to your goals? Or, are you absorbing drama and negativity that keep you from where you want to be? Are you surrounding yourself with people who will push you, challenge you, and encourage you? Or, do you let people hold you back, deflate you, or sabotage your goals and dreams? Top athletes play with the best. I encourage you to be your best and surround yourself with the best.

****

Another very popular phrase from Tony Robbins that has really impacted my heart is, "Life is not happening to you; it is happening for you." We are not *victims*, and we can't wallow or stay stuck because of events in our lives. This doesn't imply that we shouldn't have sympathy, empathy, or grieve what life sometimes throws our way, but rather that those events can empower you.

This mindset shift depends on how we look at situations, it does not negate them. When I first attended Tony Robbins' *Unleash The Power Within* experience, he shared that if he had not experienced the abuse and challenges he did, he wouldn't be the person he is today. All of his stories and experiences could have led him to feel guilty, shameful, or worst of all, a victim. Instead, they empowered him, fueled him, and drove him to change not only his life but millions of others as well.

Instead of telling himself, "No one will love me," or "Things like this will always happen to me," he actually decided to find gratitude for the events so he would never be the same and never treat others that way. I remember Tony telling a story about his businesses losing a significant amount of money at one time. Instead of getting angry or blaming someone, he came back stronger, learned more skills, and his businesses significantly increased in revenue. Again, he exemplified that the event wasn't happening *to* him but rather *for* him, to teach him something and propel him forward to something greater.

When I think about my own life, I could have taken a path toward self-destruction, fulfilling a "story" that was a lie, and staying stuck. I could have blamed the world for what happened to me. Instead, I chose a path that allows me to learn, grow, and come back stronger than ever. I made a choice to take every knockdown as an opportunity to rise up better, clearer, and more driven than I was before.

I made a choice that every time someone told me "You can't _ _ _ _ _ _," I found a way to say, "I did." Much like Tony, I adopted a mentality that every ounce of abuse shaped me to take a stance for others. Every bit of disappointment, hurt, and pain I endured was only fuel for me to be the person I am today—an inspiration for others, a voice for others, and a catalyst for change.

I love the saying, "Without the storm, the rainbow can't shine." I will never forget the first time I heard this and how strongly it resonated with me. This was a light-switch moment when I saw that I became a leader because of the challenges I overcame. If I didn't need to rise up and get off the curb any time someone tried to put me there, I wouldn't be who I am today.

****

Ask yourself: What challenging events can you now look back on and say, *That happened for me?* Can you look back and feel grateful for what you learned, what it showed you, or how it got you to where you are today? Maybe this was in a relationship. Maybe it was a financial decision. I would love to challenge you that when you want to slide into a "shame-and-blame" mindset, stop and remind yourself, "Life is happening for me, not to me." I bet you will feel the situation much differently than before.

Lisa

Lisa Nichols is an incredibly inspiring woman who coined the phrase: "Conviction and convenience don't live on the same block." One of the reasons I've always related to Lisa is because she takes action—massive action. We've all heard the phrase, "Life happens outside of your comfort zone," or, "We grow when we get uncomfortable," but Lisa truly exemplifies and teaches that truth.

Lisa completely transformed her own life, which is why she can now share the knowledge she has with others. Lisa is the founder and CEO of Motivating The Masses Inc., a personal and business development company. She teaches her unique approach to achieving your full potential in all areas of life. Lisa's teachings regarding the law of attraction are also featured in the best-selling book *The Secret*.

I am sure you understand why she has been such a force in my life, someone I follow, someone who inspires me, and someone who I can look at and say, *If she can, I can—and so can you!*

I first heard Lisa speak at a conference in Las Vegas. She said something that completely perked up my ears. "Fear is not meant to stop you; it's meant to wake you up... to keep you up at night preparing and prepping for your goals." I agree! So often we fear failure or what others will think when that fear really needs to be the fuel of where you're going, what you want to achieve.

Lisa chatted about being willing to *understand* your story but not *live* in your story. I can recall her saying, "I'm not successful in spite of my story; I'm successful *because* of my story!" This is so similar to Tony Robbins' principle of life happening *for* you, not to you. What I hear is, "Wake up, don't be a victim, stop feeling sorry for yourself! Get up, shake it off, and do something about it! Forgive, grow, and go help someone else!"

Lisa shared how we often wait until things are perfect or certain details are in place before taking action, but we need to take action when things are imperfect. She explained how she made a lot of great decisions but also how many more mistakes she made along the way. When I hear her talk about this, I think of famous failures. No one learns as much from their successes as we learn from the lessons along the way. Thomas Edison is known for inventing the lightbulb, not the 1,000 other attempts where he failed trying to invent the lightbulb. Sometimes we focus on where it wasn't perfect, not on what we learned from it. We need to fail forward! Progress is progress, even if it's imperfect. We just need to keep moving forward, even—and especially—when we fail!

Lisa teaches four quadrants of holistic success: Spirituality, Health and Wellness, Finance and Business, and Relationships. I think so often we get wrapped up in one area of life, such as losing weight or saving money, that we neglect the synergy and interconnectedness of these components.

Stop and ask yourself: How could I have a healthy relationship if I am constantly worried about money? How could I have ideal health if I am overworked?

The quadrants go hand in hand. I've met some incredibly wealthy individuals who are incredibly unhealthy. I've met some people who are so in love or have the best social calendar, but they have nothing in savings and are buried in debt.

Having the ideal life or "have it all" lifestyle means finding success and balance in all areas. I am a goal setter (no surprise), and many times throughout the year I evaluate my health and set goals for something I want to do to get better. I evaluate how much I am spending and saving, and set goals for a trip or to eliminate debt. Keeping what you want in the forefront of your mind is the best way to make sure change happens.

Jani

Earlier on, I mentioned my real-life guardian angel, the woman who opened my eyes to possibility. Jani Ehlo showed me how to dream and introduced me to the power of network marketing. What I haven't yet shared is how she made me feel, how much she believed in me, the altruism she exemplified, and most of all, what she saw in me that I hadn't yet seen in myself.

When Jani came into my life, I was a broke and broken girl. Within weeks, she had turned on a switch inside of me that gave me purpose, ignited my passion, and granted me a vision to design my life however I wanted.

This real-life angel is a giver and relentless in her servant leadership. She is a mentor who works tirelessly to assist others in reaching their goals. What stands out the most is her daily habits that I adopted, which not only taught me how to weather and manage my emotions but also leverage my mindset. How we think what we think is the most powerful component in changing how we think, manifesting what we want, and creating our ideal life. Jani taught me a number of lessons that I still continue to practice today.

I know I've said thank you before to Jani, but this is another opportunity where I know how much her voice speaking into my life changed me forever. It's because of Jani that I now see the greatness inside of me and the potential I get to share with my team and others. Thank you, Jani, for believing in me from day one, giving me hope, and igniting a grit and passion that I couldn't see before you saw it in me. You are my real-life guardian angel, and I am so grateful I met you.

Dad

I shared a great deal about some of the hardships I went through and the lessons I learned from family, but I have not shared much about my dad, the most remarkable man I've ever known. It's easy for many daughters to praise their fathers, but I am not alone when I say he is selfless, hard-working, intelligent, a remarkable leader, full of integrity, and known for doing the right thing.

He worked in his industry for more than 40 years. Shortly after his retirement, he received a Lifetime Achievement Award, which is one small testament of who he is. My dad was the *one* person who was always in my corner, unconditionally, and was always there to pick me up from the curb, literally and metaphorically. He also single-handedly is the best role model I have ever had. When I think of putting others first, it's because he exemplified it. When I think of hard work, it's because he epitomized it. When I think of honesty and trust, he solidified it.

Dad has been battling Parkinson's disease for nearly six years now, and trust me when I say that losing my knight in shining armor is so tough. While the disease has been incredibly challenging for him and hard on my stepmom and his daughters, it has been so very hard for me because, for the longest time, he was the only one I completely trusted. He was the only person I knew would always be there to protect me.

I used to tease him that I was going to get a bracelet similar to the ones that say "WWJD" (what would Jesus do?) But mine would say, "What would Dad do?" because his wisdom would always guide me in the right direction. For more than 30 years he took care of me, unconditionally, and these days I take care of him. When I want to be weak I find strength, because without a doubt, I know that I am who I am today because of him.

GETTING OFF YOUR CURB

Up until now, much of this has been my story and what I've learned that I want to share with you. Since you're reading this, there's a good chance you have your own curb, your own place where you're stuck. My hope is that you see my story as a launching pad to get off your own curb.

You may be thinking, "I know I need to get off my curb, but *how*? How do I get off and stay off my curb?"

I don't know your exact situation. I wish we could sit down for a great chat over a cup of coffee so I could ask you all about where you grew up, what you dream of doing, and as we lean in more, hear you share about *your* curb. Maybe we'll get to have that chat someday, but for now, here's what's worked for me, and my hope is that it will help you find what works for you.

Daily Rituals

One of the trends I've seen from anyone who's successful, whether physically, financially, or publicly, is the common theme of having daily rituals. I remember reading Lisa Nichols was once asked during an interview, "What's one daily practice that ensures you handle disappointments well every time?"

Her advice was to stand in front of a mirror every day for a month and complete three different sentences in seven different ways each:

- "I am proud that I..."
- "I forgive you for..."
- "I commit to you that..."

How would you feel, if every day for 31 days, you told yourself seven things you were proud of, seven things you forgave yourself for, and seven commitments you make to yourself?

This is another example of how we condition our mindsets and ultimately set ourselves up for what we want. This helps us find ways to release memories and moments from the past that don't serve us and then develop a strong, gritty mindset. These habits are wonderful with no *wrong* way of doing this.

I found strength in my acceptance speech, while others might find strength in positive affirmation cards. I wrote letters to get old feelings out, even though they were never mailed, while someone else might actually want to call someone and apologize. The point is to develop the ritual and make it your own.

Strength to Apologize

Another lesson I learned is having the strength to sincerely apologize. I was so defensive for many years and so guarded that even if I was in the wrong, I struggled to take ownership. I think I used to feel that if I admitted guilt, it would imply that I did it intentionally, so I found myself in a pattern of making excuses or justifications instead of just owning what happened.

I also have found myself stretched way too thin, and inevitably letting everyone down because I was trying to do too much at once. The "I'm not good enough" story perpetuates this for me because my pattern of wanting to please others, to make sure I exceeded expectations, and not wanting to let people down often led to over commitments.

Does that sound familiar? I found strength in apologizing when necessary and being vulnerable. I also realized that I grew closer to people as I came out of my shell and explained to them how I was thinking and feeling. I found the more I let people in, the more grace I give myself, as well as the grace I feel given to me. What sounds so simple is so powerful. This practice provides a level of vulnerability that friends and family connect with, and gives you permission to not be perfect, not to be a superhero, but to give yourself grace, just like you would give anyone else.

Gratitude

My daily gratitude practice gives me significant benefits. We all have stuff going on, but I also truly believe we always have something to be thankful for. A few years ago when I had $17 to my name, sitting on the floor of an empty apartment, I found gratitude for all of the jobs I had because I knew some money was coming in. While I was sad in the past for not having the relationship I wanted, I was grateful for my girlfriends, my family, and my peers who brought joy and happiness to my heart.

I started this practice in 2013 and have done it ever since. Every morning I write out a minimum of 10 things I'm grateful for and why I am grateful for them simply to raise my vibration and consciously shift my focus to joy and gratitude instead of comparison, resentment, frustration, or other emotions that don't serve me or others.

It is one thing to say I am grateful for my health, but when you can really *feel* gratitude, and understand all of the blessings for it, your focus will shift. Even when times are tough, I find gratitude. Here's a question if you're striving for more in your life: "If you're not grateful for what you have now, how could you ever be given more?"

Intentions

Another daily habit is to state my intentions for the day and write them down. If you've ever taken a yoga class or even a group fitness class, often that instructor will ask at the beginning: "What is your intention for the workout?" When the workout gets tough, we get back to that intention.

When I write out my intentions for the day, it guides my attention, assists my production goals, eliminates distractions, and keeps me clear on my purpose. It is so easy to find ourselves busy without necessarily accomplishing anything. It's so easy to get wrapped up in the hustle and bustle that we lose sight of our passions.

My daily intentions ground me and guide me. Since I'm a goal setter and track my goals, and you may as well, it's important to note that goal setting is different from setting intentions. Intentions are almost like a road map for your mind or schedule. When I set an intention, it may be to show up positive, joyful, full of light, and ready to give my energy to the world, to empower others, to support others, and to be a catalyst of change for someone looking for a solution that will change the trajectory of their life.

An intention might be to not sweat any of the small stuff and to be fully present and full of gratitude every step of the day. On the other hand, goal setting might be an amount of closed business I want to do in a month or a certain mile pace I want to achieve while running. Having the clarity and vision of how you behave and the choices you make is the directional map to achieving the goals you strive for.

If you ever want to know what's important to you, evaluate your calendar and your bank statements. When my intentions are clear, I make better choices physically, emotionally, financially, and socially.

Fitness

Our bodies were designed to move. I am a huge advocate of the psychological benefits of exercise, and never take my health for granted. I know that I am happier, less anxious, and more creative when I make time to sweat. Regardless of whether I am in hot yoga, at spin class, or out for a run, I start my day with endorphins, an elevated heart rate, and thankfulness for a healthy body.

While none of these are complicated in nature, the key is consistency. Results do not happen overnight, but they do come with diligence and habits. I once heard a friend say, "The minute you stop striving for everything you want, everything you don't want shows up."

When I get lazy with my gratitude, I find myself focusing on what's not working in my life instead of what is. When I deviate from my intention statements, my business stops growing and sometimes declines. I don't take major lulls from exercise, but when I miss a day or two, even from being ill or traveling, not only do I not *feel* as good, but I notice I am crankier, more irritable, and accomplish less throughout the day.

People say they don't have time to exercise, but I would argue that those who do exercise get more done. We all have different ways of creating habits that aid in having a positive mindset or affect how we show up every day. I encourage you to create your healthy habits and stick with them. Over time, I assure you, you will feel better, enjoy healthier relationships, and find more of what you *do* want showing up in your life.

Determination

Determination is not necessarily something you can *do;* however, it is who I am, and absolutely a characteristic that has led to my success. I can recall late nights after going out and being hungry when everything was closed, finding the *one* pizza place open that would deliver at 4 a.m. Having determination means denying the temporary satisfaction of yummy pizza and making a better choice, going to bed after a light, healthier snack, is what sets the tone for how you feel in the morning.

Determination is also the pivot point for so much success. My first book, *Why Can't is a Four-Letter Word*, goes into great depth about how to get out of your way and beat expectations. Relentless pursuit, grit, and perseverance are critical characteristics to overcome obstacles and find success. When I think of famous failures such as Oprah, who was told she was unfit for TV, or Walt Disney, whose business partner mocked his dream, I think about how determined they must have been.

When I think about the resistance I had to overcome to graduate from high school, it was my determination that carried me through. When I think about what it takes to be a top earner in a network marketing company, determination is the fuel. When I decided to write a book (when I didn't even have a blog), determination led the pursuit. Many friends and family have said to me, "You were determined even as a little kid," or, "I've never met anyone as determined as you."

You can't teach determination; you only have to know how to *activate* it. Determination resides in all of us, and my hope and wish is for you to turn it on! Get after what you want and don't let anyone or anything stand in your way!

Vision

My vision is clear for myself and for others. My vision for myself is to never be on the curb again, to follow my agreements, and to activate all of the tools and healing keys I know to play big and shine bright in this world.

My vision for others is to help them find self-love, embody forgiveness for others, and identify their self-limitations so they can do anything they want! My story is not pretty in all areas, but it is why I am who I am. My goal is to find others who have an amazing story and help them show how their story is not something that should hold them back but become a catalyst for igniting them to be more, do more, and shine brighter! From the time I wake up daily, or when I am dreaming big about life to come in the following decades, I have passion, gratitude, and clarity.

You hold this potential too. You can find what ignites your passion, what gets you off the curb. That is what will guide you to stay off the curb and start reaching your greatest potential.

FINDING YOUR PLACE: Off the Curb and Over the Rainbow

When I look back at my life today, three major events led to perpetual fight-or-flight behavior and left me on the curb: childhood ridicule, my best friend's murder, and repeated bad relationships.

When I think of how I overcame that response, I am confident about three major moments: my trip to New Zealand, finding my journey with health and wellness, and taking the feedback and lessons from mentors and coaches who wanted the best for me, specifically Jani and Lisa. They say good things come in threes, and today I am so grateful for an incredible global business with my health and wellness network marketing company, close and special relationships with my friends and family, and for falling in love with my best friend... my real-life soul mate.

The older I get, the more I realize how all of the pieces of my life puzzle are falling into place, exactly as they should. My dad used to sing *Somewhere Over the Rainbow* to us as little girls. Later on, a rendition was played at my Aunt Patti's funeral, the champion who was in my corner as an early teen. My mom thinks of her mom every time she sees a rainbow, and personally, I know the storm has passed and the sun is shining every time the colorful arcs light up the sky.

Life has never been nor will it ever be perfect, but I've learned to dance in the rain. I may not ever know why Mary's killer did what he did. I may not ever understand why I was the endless scapegoat or source of mockery as a child or why certain loved ones didn't stand up for me. I might not ever know why I was cheated on, lied to, or betrayed by multiple men.

What I do know is that Mary taught me to never take anything or anyone for granted, to always speak your truth, and to be authentic. Losing Mary will always be a piece of my story, and she will always have a piece of my heart, but I choose not to stay in fear, not to obsess about why, but embrace who she was and the lessons I learned. It would be easy to stay mad about what happened more than 20 years ago, but anger was keeping me from the people I love and preventing a closeness I desired.

I let go of truly understanding why I was so ridiculed and I know I may not ever receive an apology; however, I found grace for other people having a *story*, and I found the gratitude for the woman I have become. If I hold on to resentment, it seems the only person that continues to hurt is me. I've never condoned what happened, but I forgave. I have forgiven everyone so we can have the relationships we do today, and most of all, so that I no longer carry the pain and agony I did for so long.

For a long time I also carried bitterness from men I dated who hurt me, but today my heart is happy that none of them worked out so that I could end up with my life partner. I met a man who is so caring, supportive, loving, genuine, and honest. Sometimes I wonder if I hadn't experienced such heartache, would I feel so much gratitude or value him this much? Sometimes going through heartache teaches you a level of love and appreciation you may not have ever known.

I know what it's like to be mistreated, and while some might say, "Lauren, this is the way it should be," for me, having a kind, giving, supportive, and patient man was not something I ever experienced before now. I will always cherish that he gets up early to have coffee ready for me, opens car doors, and rearranges his schedule to be at events that are important to me. I can't put into words what it means to have someone carry my suitcases upstairs after a long trip, and tickle my hair or rub my shoulders after a long day. The most important part is he loves me just the way I am. Whether I am dolled up for a night on the town or unshowered and a hot mess from the gym, he sees me and loves me.

I found someone I can be playful and romantic with, and I feel at ease with being *me*. For the first time, I completely trust, let my guard down, am vulnerable, and am completely myself. If you're still looking for your soul mate, please don't settle. Believe in your heart your perfect match is out there and continue to work on yourself, be the best partner you can be, and that person will come. Listen to feedback from others who are trying to help you—and don't overlook surprises because you never know when the timing will be just right. I was lonely for a long time, but I wouldn't trade it to find someone sooner because I wasn't ready, and I wouldn't have found the amazing man that I did.

Some days I feel accomplished and very proud of all I have done, and just like anyone else, some days I am too critical, find myself comparing, or wonder if what I am doing is enough. I am almost 36 years old, and while in love, I am not yet married, and while I want to be a mom so badly, I still do not have children. I can easily get caught up in the rat race of what others have and what I don't, but I choose to trust the process, trust the timing, and most of all, trust what is somewhere over the rainbow.

Letting go of what you can't control is never easy, but I also believe trying to control what you can't control is harder. Comparison is the thief of joy, so stop worrying about everyone else and keep your eyes on what's ahead of you. You will find your place off the curb. Holding onto the past doesn't serve anyone, so embrace what the future holds, and when in doubt, know that multiple hues of love and light are readily available for you to write your story ... just the way you want.

EPILOGUE: Thank You...

Wow, thank you so much for reading this far. It's incredible that you took the time to walk with me through my story. That's amazing, and I am so grateful for you.

The story doesn't end here though. It continues with you loving life, embracing gratitude for all of the many blessings and lessons you're navigating, enjoying every day, and paying it forward.

For me, I'm thankful that your future is now off the curb. Your decision to get off the curb and stay off the curb is what will change your life and the lives of so many because you said, "Yes!"

I see such an incredible future for you where your lover and friends and family and co-workers and even complete strangers sense the vibe of goodness and light radiating from you. I hear the joy and laughter in your life because you're no longer stuck on the curb.

My journey to ignite healthy rebellion is to encourage YOU to be the best version of you, to let go of the word *can't*, and ultimately to step into your greatness. That's what it means to be free. That's what it means to be truly off the curb. Your best days are still ahead, and I can't wait to celebrate and step into the future with you. Let's leave the curb behind and live amazing lives with love, hope, passion, and purpose that others can't wait to ask us about.

XOXO,

Lauren

RESOURCES

- CliftonStrengths assessment (formerly Clifton StrengthsFinder): gallupstrengthscenter.com
- Enneagram: enneagraminstitute.com
- Lisa Foster: parillume.com

ACKNOWLEDGEMENTS

- To Amy Collette, who gave countless hours, reviews, and attention to detail, and also provided lovingly direct advice in order to make a dream come true.
- To Jon Cook, for listening, editing, and collectively organizing my stories and ideas into one, while continuously providing encouragement and belief every step of the way.
- To Lisa Foster, for cracking my code, empowering me, and guiding me through the program that assisted me in letting go of the past, rising into my purpose, loving myself, and ultimately, allowing others to love me too.
- To Jani Ehlo, my real-life guardian angel, who showed me what life could be like with grit, hard work, and servant leadership. My entire life improved because of the vision you saw for me.
- To my family, my entire family... because of all of you, I am who I am.
- To the love of my life, Ryan Friarson, who has only ever supported me, loved me, elevated me, and continues to unconditionally stand in my corner in the aspiration of my dreams and goals.

ABOUT THE AUTHOR

Lauren Danielle is an industry leader in health and wellness, a commander in personal development, a nationally recognized speaker and trainer, and the author of *Why Can't Is A Four-Letter Word*. Lauren's greatest passion is helping people break through physical, financial, emotional, and time barriers in order to live their fullest life possible.

She has undergraduate degrees in both psychology and sociology, dual master's degrees, over 15 years of experience in both her coaching and clinical practices, and has mentored and advised a variety of professionals, including top executives, entrepreneurs, and passionate individuals who want to make an impact or leave a legacy for others.

Lauren is an incredibly inspiring writer, speaker, and leader, pushing you to reach what you once thought was impossible.

Lauren is so easy to relate to, you will find your story in her voice and be compelled to go out and take action in your own life!

Connect with Lauren at:
lifewithlaurendanielle.com/
facebook.com/lifewithlaurendanielle
instagram.com/lifewithlaurendanielle
linkedin.com/in/lifewithlaurendanielle/

42830062R00104

Made in the USA
San Bernardino, CA
11 July 2019